THE OXFORD DEBATE

ON THE

TEXTUAL CRITICISM OF THE NEW TESTAMENT

HELD AT NEW COLLEGF
ON MAY 6, 1897

WITH A PREFACI
EXPLANATORY OF THE
RIVAL SYSTEMS

Prebendary Edward Miller

Edited for Publication by H. D. Williams, M.D., Ph.D.

LONDON: GEORGE BELL & SONS OXFORD: JAMES PARKER. & CO.
CAMBRIDGE: DEIGHTON BELL. & CO.

1897

Reprinted by the Dean Burgon Society with Comments
2009

The Dean Burgon Society

Box 354 Collingswood, New Jersey 08108

www.Dean BurgonSociety.org

April 2009

ISBN 978-0-9822230-1-7

Published by:

THE OLD PATHS PUBLICATIONS, INC.

142 Gold Flume Way

Cleveland, Georgia, U.S.A.

Web: www.theoldpathspublications.com

E-mail: TOP@theoldpathspublications.com

BIBLE FOR TODAY NUMBER #3397

Web: www.biblefortoday.org

E-mail: bft@biblefortoday.org

Dean Burgon Society

Box 354

Collingswood, New Jersey 08108

www.Dean BurgonSociety.org

1.0

1 Peter 1:23-25 ²³ "Being born again, not of corruptible seed, but of incorruptible, by the word of God, which liveth and abideth for ever. ²⁴ For all flesh *is* as grass, and all the glory of man as the flower of grass. The grass withereth, and the flower thereof falleth away: ²⁵ But the word of the Lord endureth for ever. And this is the word which by the gospel is preached unto you."

Matthew 24:35 "Heaven and earth shall pass away, but my words shall not pass away."

CONTENTS

---

[1] British spelling (Editor, HDW)

FORWARD

About This Book

This book, *The Oxford Debate on the Textual Criticism of the New Testament,* was compiled by Edward Miller from a debate in which he was a participant at New College in 1897. The book is reprinted by the Dean Burgon Society (DBS), a non-profit organization, as a service to God's people. It will serve well as an introductory primer on the debate surrounding modern textual criticism. The DBS does not agree with every point of every speaker supporting Dean Burgon.

Edward Miller was an understudy, student, close associate, and defender of Dean John William Burgon. He supported the Dean's principles and approach to the defense of the Traditional Text of the New Testament, but he was not as vigorous as the Dean in his defense. Mr. Miller continued the defense of Dean Burgon after the Dean's death.

The Dean Burgon Society, under the leadership of Dr. D. A. Waite, Th.D., Ph.D., who has been its President for over 30 years, has reprinted many of the works of Dean Burgon and Edward Miller. The works may be purchased at www.DeanBurgonSociety.org or online at Amazon by typing in the name of the book. The books reprinted are:

1. *The Revision Revised*
2. *The Traditional Text of the Holy Gospels*
3. *The Causes of Corruption of the Traditional Text*
4. *The Last Twelve Verses of Mark*
5. *Inspiration and Interpretation*

6. *A Guide to the Textual Criticism of the New Testament* by Edward Miller

7. *Scrivener's Annotated Greek New Testament*

Other books published by the DBS include:

8. *Forever Settled* by Dr. Jack Moorman

9. *Ten Reason Why The Dean Burgon Society Deserves Its Name* by Dr. D. A. Waite

10. *The Oxford Debate on the Textual Criticism of the New Testament* by Edward Miller

11. *8,000 Differences Between the N.T. Greek Words of the King James Bible and the Modern Versions* by Dr. Jack A. Moorman

This book, *The Oxford Debate,* is another work by Edward Miller initially organized and printed in 1897. The formatting of the original book was changed to accommodate modern fonts and organization. The wording was not changed. Please note the British spelling of words is often slightly different. Occasionally, headings were added for clarity and footnotes were placed in the work for understanding. They will be noted by a parenthesis such as (HDW) following the heading or footnote added. Definitions and common abbreviations have been listed at the beginning. A table of contents and an index has been added for convenience along with an explanatory forward.

Duplicity Amongst Modernists

The reader should be aware that modern textual criticism has continued to present a duplicitous approach to the New Testament. Many modern textual critics have besmirched the principles of textual criticism laid down by Brooke Foss Westcott (1825-1903) and Fenton John Anthony Hort (1828-1892) (W/H); yet, they have not abandoned the basic text constructed by W/H. For example, Kurt Aland, the well known German textual critic who is heralded by many as the best modern day textual critic, said:

"The age of Westcott and Hort... is definitely over!"[2]

K. W. Clark said:

"The textual history that the Westcott-Hort text represents is no longer tenable in the light of newer discoveries and fuller textual analysis. In the effort to construct a congruent history, our failure suggests that we have lost the way, that we have reached a dead end, and that only a new and different insight will enable us to break through."[3]

Even so, the use of the text constructed by Westcott and Hort from primarily two corrupted manuscripts (B and Aleph), for all intents and purposes, remains the essential text behind modern versions of the Bible. Today this text is called the United Bible Society (UBS), Nestle-Aland (NA), or the Critical Text (CT). Furthermore, the UBS, NA, or CT remains the text selected by most translators and publishers of the New Testament. This is inexplicable. It demonstrates the extreme unfounded prejudice for the Critical Text.

---

[2] H. D. Williams, M.D., Ph.D., *The Lie That Changed The Modern World* (The Old Paths Publications, Cleveland, GA, originally published by Bible For Today, Collingswood, NJ, 2004) p. 215.

[3] Ibid. p. 215-216.

Recent Discoveries Ignored

Furthermore, the continuing pejorative comments about the Traditional Text/Textus Receptus (TT/TR) are baseless. They are unfounded in light of the recent discoveries and documentation by researchers such as Herman Hoskier and Jack Moorman.[4] Here are some comments about Herman Hoskier and some quotes from his book by Cecil J. Carter:

> "It is high time that the bubble of Codex B should be pricked." H. Hoskier "Codex B and its Allies" P.1 Vol. 1 Preface. Hoskier, a distinguished scholar, in a magnificent rebuttal of the outrageous claims made in favour of Vaticanus and Sinaiticus, has published over 900 pages of scholarly refutation; and exposure of the erroneous claims of the scholars who have believed, without verification, that these were the "oldest and best." [He said: "I present therefore an indictment against the manuscript B (Vaticanus) and against Westcott and Hort, subdivided into hundreds of separate counts. I do not believe that the jurymen who will ultimately render a verdict have ever had the matter presented to them formally, legally, and in proper detail." H. Hoskier Codex B. Vol. 1 P.1 Preface In his remarkable analysis Hoskier directs our attention to the fact that scribes of "Vaticanus and Sinaiticus" had obviously taken many liberties with their texts. His comment on Hort's outlandish claim that, "Vaticanus is a neutral text", is Neutral text indeed, neutral rubbish."[5]

---

[4] See Jack A. Moorman, *8,000 Differences Between the N.T. Greek Words of the King James Bible and the Modern Versions* (Bible For Today (BFT) and The Dean Burgon Society, Collingswood, NJ, 2006); *Early Manuscripts, Church Fathers, and the Authorized Version with Manuscript Digests and Summaries* (BFT, Collingswood, NJ, 2005); Herman Hoskier, *Codex B and it Allies*.

[5] http://www.maranath.ca/OLDBEST.HTM#Hoskier

As you will discover, a great deal of attention is directed to *theoretical* or *speculative* topics by the textual critics opposed to the Traditional Text. Many of the fundamental errors of modernists have been elucidated in books written by members of the Dean Burgon Society. For example, Dr. D. A. Waite's numerous books pinpointing the errors by many Fundamentalists available at www.BibleForToday.org; Dr. David Brown's works defending the TT/TR are available at http://logosresourcepages.org; Dr. Jack A. Moorman and Dr. H. D. Williams' works are available at www.BibleForToday.org. Also, many of the works are available on Amazon by typing in the title of the work.

Dean John William Burgon, F. H. A. Scrivener, and Edward Miller, were all Byzantine-priority or Traditional Text proponents. However, their approach to defending the TT/TR varied a little.[6] Dean Burgon was vigorous in his defense; F. H. A. Scrivener's opinion fluctuated at times; and Edward Miller was not as 'strong' in his defense of the text as Dean Burgon. These differences reflect personality disparity more than academic inconsistencies. However, whatever one believes about these men and their approach to textual criticism, one thing is certain:

"The one great Fact, which especially troubles him [HORT] and his joint Editor [WESTCOTT],—(as well it may)—is *The Traditional Greek Text* of the New Testament Scriptures. Call this Text Erasmian or Complutensian,—the Text of Stephens, or of Beza, or of the Elzevirs,—call it the 'Received,' or *Traditional*

---

[6] Maurice A. Robinson, "Crossing Boundaries in New Testament Textual Criticism," (*A Journal of Biblical Textual Criticism*, 2002, Southeastern Baptist Theological Seminary, Wake Forest, North Carolina
http://rosetta.reltech.org/TC/vol07/Robinson2002.html#fn17sym

Greek Text, or whatever other name you please;—the fact remains, that **a Text *has* come down to us which is attested by a general consensus of ancient Copies, ancient Fathers, ancient Versions."**[7]

The Importance of the Peshitto

One of the favorite topics of Critical Text proponents is to argue the date of the Peshitto as you will discover in the debate to follow. The Peshitto is a great witness to the Traditional Text because:

1. All scholarly evidence points to its origin as a very early translation of the Traditional (Greek) Text. For example, it does not contain the apocryphal influence that is so common in the LXX versions that stem from Origen's (185-254 A.D.) school at Caesarea. (q.v.). The Apocrypha was placed into the corrupted version(s) after Origen moved to Caesarea, Palestine.

2. The text of the Peshitto (also Peschito or Peshitta) favors the Eastern Aramaic language (Syriac).[8] This is the language of Antioch, Syria in the apostolic and post-apostolic centuries.

3. The late date of the Peshitto assigned to the fifth century by a few Oxford and Cambridge scholars such as F. Crawford Burkitt, a palaeography lecturer at Cambridge

---

[7] Dean John William Burgon, *The Revision Revised* (The Dean Burgon Society Press, Collingswood, NJ, originally published, 1883, reprinted 2000) 269.

[8] Jack Moorman, *Forever Settled* (Dean Burgon Society, Collingswood, NJ) pp. 34-35.

(1904), is out of favor.[9] He gave undue credit to the Bishop of Edessa, Rabbula. Burkitt said:

> "Our oldest MSS. of the Peshitta date from about the middle of the fifth century, and the earliest piece of contemporary biography which we possess is the life of Rabbula. Let us therefore start from the episcopate of Rabbula, Bishop of Edessa from 411 to 435 A.D."

4. Dean Burgon reported in *Revision Revised:*

> "thus, the Peschito Syriac and the Old Latin version are believed to have been executed in the IInd century. "It is no stretch of imagination" (wrote Bp. Ellicott in 1870,) "to suppose that portions of the Peschito might have been in the hands of S. John, or the Old Latin represented the current views of the Roman Christians of the IInd century."[10]

5. Further corruptions of the Peshitto (meaning simple) or Syrian Peschito took place at Origin's Caesarean school (3rd century) and later the Philoxian (508), Harclean (616), and Jerusalem Syriac (5th century) corruptions and revisions took place. There are many references in the literature to these works.

6. The disagreement over the Peshitto centers on the dates of

---

[9] F. Crawford Burkitt, *Early Eastern Christianity, St. Margaret's Lectures, 1904, on the Syriac-Speaking Church* (John Murray, London, 1904) p. 39-78, particularly p. 48-49; Jack Moorman, *Forever Settled*, p. 66.

[10] Dean Burgon, *Revision Revised* (The Dean Burgon Society, Collingswood, NJ, reprinted 2000) p. 9.

the Lewis Codex and the Curetonian Codex. The Syrian Curetonian Codex of the gospels is dated in the 5th century by William Cureton. The Lewis Codex, an early Syrian church lectionary, was found by Agnes Smith Lewis (1843-1926) at Saint Catherine Monastery in the Arabian Desert. Its date is uncertain. Dr. Harper said:

> "The value of the Lewis codex has been much overrated in the judgment of Dr. Resch. He holds it to be later than the Curetonian, which with Baethgen he assigns to the middle of the third century."[11]

As far as the Lucian Text is concerned, most careful scholars agree that the TR/TT did not originate with any Lucian revision. In the following quote, the author inappropriately uses "Lucian" for the TR/TT (q.v.).

> "[Adam] Mez agrees with the conclusions reached by others. namely. that the *Velus Latinus* often agrees with the Lucian readings, and in many cases with the Peshitto. Then, too. the author is convinced that the basis or **original source of the Lucian text is considerably older than Lucian**."[12] (HDW, my emphasis)

The Reason for the Reprint

By reprinting this work, it is hoped that a greater

---

[11] William R. Harper, "The Biblical World" (The University of Chicago Press, *New* Series, Vol. VIII, July-December, 1896) p. 514.
[12] Ibid. p. 59.

understanding of the issues will be gained. Too much theory has been carried into modern textual criticism from the false philosophy and pseudoscience of the ages past. The evidence continues to accumulate that:

1.   Every Word of our Lord is true to the "jot and tittle" (Mat. 4:4, 5:17-18).
2.   The Words are forever settled in heaven (Psa. 119:89).
3.   The Words shall never pass away (Mat. 24:35).
4.   The Words are our rule or Canon (2 Cor. 10:13, Gal. 6:16).
5.   The Words endureth forever (1Pe. 1:24-25).

There is no question that we have all of the Words God said He would preserve (Psa. 12:6-7). What is this chatter heard around the world today that all we have is a message from God that is not preserved perfectly in the Hebrew, Aramaic, and Greek Texts behind the King James Bible? It is echoes from the past by misled and heretical men.[13] See for yourself in the debate that follows.

The Question Submitted for the Debate

The question presented for the debate was:

<u>"The question to be determined is, what are the scientific principles to be applied in the definition of the true text of the Bible?"</u>

The debaters (opponents and responders) were:

---

[13] Pastor D. A. Waite, Th.D., Ph.D., *The Heresies of Westcott and Hort* (Bible For Today, Collingswood, NJ, revised 2004, B.F.T. #595.

1.   Moderator: **William Ince** (1825-1910) was a British theologian. Ince was educated at King's College School and Lincoln College, Oxford, where he took first-class honours in Literae Humaniores (BA 1846, MA 1849, DD 1878). He was a Fellow of Exeter College, Oxford from 1847 to 1878 (Sub Rector 1857-78) and Regius Professor of Divinity in the University of Oxford and Canon Residentiary of Christ Church, Oxford from 1878 until his death (Sub Dean 1901 to death). (Wikipedia)

2.   **Prebendary Edward Miller**, M.A., Rector of Bucknell, Oxon. (1825-1901) was a 19th century textual critic and understudy, student, and defender of John Burgon, Dean of Chichester, and co-author *of A Textual Commentary upon the Holy Gospels;* largely from the use of Materials, and Mainly on the Text, left by the Late John William Burgon, B. D., Dean of Chichester. Part I. St. Matthew; Division I. i.-xiv (London: George Bell & Sons, 1899).

3.   **William Sanday**, 1843–1920, English theologian and biblical scholar. He was professor of exegesis (1883–95) at Oxford and from 1895 to 1919 Lady Margaret professor of divinity and canon of Christ Church, Oxford. The Lady Margaret professor of divinity chair was founded in 1502 by the mother of Henry VII. He was joint editor of the *Variorum Bible* (1880) and won acceptance for new methods of New Testament study among Anglican clergy. Besides commentaries, his many writings include *The Authorship and Historical Character of the Fourth Gospel* (1872), *The Gospels in the Second Century* (1876), and *The New Testament Background* (1918). (Robinson). It is said of him:

> "The five elements which Mr. Bartlett names as characterizing Dr. Sanday's work, and which give him and his writings so wide and strong an influence, are: Scientific method, sobriety of judgment, width of erudition, exactitude of scholarship, and lucidity of

style. These qualities, singly and in combination, make him the worthy successor of Bishop Lightfoot and Dr. Hort."[14]

4.   **Rev. G. H. Gwilliam** (c 1892) Fellow of Hertford, Oxford. He was the author of several books and important articles; particularly on the Peshitto. Dean Burgon complimented him in *The Causes of the Corruption of the Traditional Text of the Holy Gospels* (page 4).

5.   **Rev. Albert Bonus**, Pembroke, Oxford, Scholar of Hertford 1879, Pembroke, a Hall-Houghton Prizeman in 1879.

6.   **Rev. A. C. Headlam**, (1886-1909) All Souls College, Oxford, Durham and Sedbergh Schools; Trinity College, Cambridge (Scholar and Members' Prize). BA 1849; MA 1852; adeundem, Durham, 1868. Deacon, 1849; priest, 1851; Curate of Knebworth, Herts, 1851-1852; Wycliffe, Yorks, 1852-1854; Vicar of Whorlton, Durham, 1854-1876; St Oswald's, Durham, 1876-1896; Gainford, Durham, 1896-1901; Proc. Diocese Durham, 1880-1885; Hon. Canon of Durham, 1901.[15]

Please be aware that many spelling differences exist between Britain and America. In addition, the Greek text in this work was transliterated on the first occurrences of the Greek words in the debate by the editor for the DBS.

The chart to follow on the next several pages may be of some assistance as the debate is studied.

---

[14] Ibid. (The Biblical World, p. 58)
[15] http://www.headlam.me.uk/html_pages/headlam_A.htm

Points Argued In the Debate		
TOPIC	**TR/TT Supporters**	**CT Supporters**
Several Recensions of the NT Text	Denied	Supported
Oldest MSS are best	Denied	Supported
Conflation of TR/TT	Denied	Supported
Families of groups of MSS	Denied (allowance for some grouping)	Supported
Hardest and shortest readings best	Denied	Supported
Vatican and Sinaitic MSS corrupted	Supported	Denied with qualifications
Early on, the W/H system of criticism supported by many	Denied	Not addressed
Mass (number) of MSS important	Supported	Denied
Testimony of MSS, Versions, and Fathers important	Supported	Denied
Council of Nicea's statement: *"Let ancient customs prevail"* important	Supported	Denied
Uncorrupted descendent genealogy of TR/TT from Caesarea to Constantinople to Europe	Supported	Denied
Early MSS deteriorated secondary to fragile papyrus use	Supported	Ignored

Existence of a Neutral Text	Denied	Supported
Alexandrian Texts corrupted	Supported	Denied
Alleged "Western Text" MSS exhibit too many differences to be called a family	Supported	Denied
Eusebius Produced the Sinaitic and Vatican MSS	Supported	Denied
Old Latin MSS favor primarily the TR/TT 5 to 4	Supported	Ignored
History of MSS a significant problem	Supported	Denied
Great respect for B and Aleph	Denied	Supported
Vaticanus and Sinaiticus MSS produced in Italy secondary to "Istrael" spelling	Denied (perhaps copies were made there)	Supported
Single MSS more important as original than all the mass of MSS, etc.	Denied	Supported
Authority of the church in the matter of Words	Supported	Denied
Peshitto is a revision of an earlier text	Greatly Doubted	Supported
Revision of the Greek Text grew over time	Denied	Supported

Peshitto is "the sheet answer" to the early text	Denied	Supported

H. D. Williams, M.D., Ph.D., Editor for the DBS,
A Dean Burgon Society Vice-President,
For Pastor D. A. Waite, Th.D., Ph.D.,
President of the Dean Burgon Society

"For the LORD is good; his mercy is everlasting; and his truth endureth to all generations." Psalms 100:5

ABBREVIATIONS & DEFINTIONS

A = uncial manuscript Alexandrinus at the British Library in London dated 450.

Aleph = (א) manuscript kept in London at the British Library thought to be from the 4th century (350 A.D.). A few leaves (pages) are in Lepzig; Alexandrian type.

Apost. = a lectionary of the Acts and Epistles.

B = the uncial manuscript thought to be from the 4th century (350 A.D.) housed in the Vatican; Alexandrian type.

C = Ephraemi uncial housed in France at the National Library; dated 450 A.D.

Cursive = handwritten manuscripts in small letters or script much like one would write today. Also called minuscules. They are usually numbered, e.g. 1-3,000.

D = uncial codex Bezae housed at Cambridge in the UK.

e.g. = for example (L).

E.M. = Edward Miller

Evst = a lectionary of the Gospels.

i.e. = that is (L).

L = Regis uncial manuscript of the NT from the 8th century kept at the National Library of France; Alexandrian type.

Latin a, b, c, etc. = Latin manuscripts.

MS = a manuscript; usually the British place a period after the abbreviation. We do not.

MSS = manuscripts; usually the British place a period after the abbreviation. We do not.

Palimpsest = a manuscript scrapped off and used again; also called a rescriptus.

papyri = manuscripts prepared on a paper- like material from reeds; usually designated with a "P"

q.v. = which see (in this work)

TT/TR = Traditional Text/Textus Receptus

Uncial = capital letter manuscript usually designated with a capital letter.

viz. = namely (L).

W/H = Westcott & Hort

Psalms 12:6-7 [6] "The words of the LORD *are* pure words: *as* silver tried in a furnace of earth, purified seven times. [7] Thou shalt keep them, O LORD, thou shalt preserve them from this generation for ever."

PREFACE

By Edward Miller

THE debate, of which the following pages contain a report, was the result of an offer courteously made by the Rev. Dr. Sanday, Lady Margaret Professor of Divinity, when I asked him whether those who are devoted to the study of Theology in Oxford would be ready to hear an explanation from me of the system of Textual Criticism advocated by the late Dean Burgon and myself, in order to the removal of misconceptions of it.

The speeches made in the debate have been referred both in manuscript and in type to the several speakers for their approval and corrections.

The Two Systems

(Editor's addition of the heading, HDW)

In compliance with a thoughtful suggestion, the ensuing descriptions of the two present systems have been prefixed to the Report of the discussion, for the purpose of reference in the case of readers who have not a familiar acquaintance with them ready for use. And it is hoped that, taken together with the debate, they may form an easy means to many students of the Bible of learning some of the chief points in a very important study and controversy. The former (changed to latter by the editor, HDW) of these two descriptions, according to Dr. Sanday's suggestion, has been taken with the kind leave of the author from *Our Bible and the Ancient Monuments,* by Frederick G. Kenyon, M.A., D.Litt., of the British Museum.[16]

Dr. Kenyon's description has received special praise from Mr. Hort in the *Life* of his illustrious father.[17] The second (the first, HDW) I have prepared especially for this little book.

I. BURGON AND MILLER'S SYSTEM

1. The True Text.

The Great object of the Textual Criticism of the New Testament is the ascertainment of the actual or genuine words of the original autographs of the writers. Such an ascertainment can only be made with soundness and rest upon a broad basis, if all the evidence that can be collected be sifted and taken into account, and in the case of readings where the evidence is not consistent a balance be struck with all impartiality and justice. The words thus ascertained must constitute the True Text, of which the following must be the essential characteristics:

1. It must be grounded upon an exhaustive view of the evidence of Greek copies in manuscript in the first place; and in all cases where they differ so as to afford doubt, of Versions or Translations into other languages, and of Quotations from the New Testament made by Fathers and other early writers.

---

[16] Dr. Kenyon's book is available on a CD in a searchable PDF form from the Dean Burgon Society, www.DeanBurgonSociety.org. (HDW).

[17] Edward Miller is referring to the *Life and Letters of Fenton John Anthony Hort* by his son, Arthur Fenton Hort, available from Bible For Today, B.F.T. #1867. F. J. A. Hort's dates are 1828-1892. (HDW).

2. It must have descended from the actual composition of Books of the New Testament, and must thus possess the highest possible antiquity.

3. It must be the outcome, not of one stem of descent, but of many. Consentient copies, made by successive transcription in the different countries where the Holy Scriptures were used, revered, and jealously watched, must confirm and check one another.

4. The descent must be continuous, without break or failure, or it would be no real descent, but a fragmentary or stunted line of genealogy, broken up or prematurely closed.

5. The Readings, or Text, must be such as to commend themselves to the enlightened judgement[18] of Christendom.

A. The Neutral Text

Judged by these canons, the 'Neutral' Text of Dr. Hort must be rejected:

(1) It rests upon a very few documents arbitrarily selected, and is hopelessly condemned by the vast majority. It cannot reckon, therefore, number or variety. Aspiring to be the expression of the standard work of the Catholic Church, it fails in catholicity.

(2) As a collection of readings, apart from separate readings of early date, we maintain that it does not go further back than the School of Caesarea, and that in consequence it does not as a Text possess the highest antiquity.

(3) It has only one stem by hypothesis,-the probable archetype of B and Aleph (the Vatican and Sinaitic), which Dr. Hort-gratuitously in our contention-thrusts back into the second century.

---

[18] British spelling. (HDW, editor).

(4) It fails in continuity, because (a) there is thus a break or chasm in the earliest period, and (b) because by the admission of Dr. Hort himself it was superseded by the Traditional Text, by him termed 'Syrian,' before the end of the century (fourth) in which the latter Text acquired permanent expression.

(5) We contend that the Text itself is strangely blurred by numerous omissions of more or less length, including in some instances passages held by its supporters to be genuine extracts from the words or life of our Lord, and by other blemishes.

B. The Received Text

The *Textus Receptus,* which was adopted in the revival of Greek learning, though it agrees substantially with our Canons, fails under the first, which is the virtual embodiment of them all; because some of its readings are condemned by the balance struck upon all the evidence which has been assembled under the unprecedented advantages afforded in this century. There remains therefore, in accordance with the Canons already laid down, only:

C. The Traditional Text

We maintain, then, that the Traditional Text, duly ascertained according to all the evidence with all fairness of judgement,[19] will represent *the Text which issued from the pens of the writers of the New Testament and was used all over the Church; and which after contracting corruption to a large extent, perhaps in most places, was gradually purged in the main as years went on, though something is*

---

[19] British spelling. (HDW).

left still to be done.

In the ascertainment of this Text or these Readings, guidance is to be sought under seven Notes of Truth, viz.

1. Antiquity of witnesses

2. Number of witnesses

3. Variety of witnesses

4. Weight of witnesses

5. Continuity of witnesses

6. The Context of Passages

7. Internal Evidence

These Seven Notes of Truth, which are essential to the Traditional Text, sufficiently exhibit the agreement of it with the Canons laid down. In fact, coincidence with the first Canon implies coincidence with all the rest. But the age and the uninterrupted existence of the Traditional Text must be further proved.

Now Dr. Hort has admitted that the Traditional Text has existed ever since the later years of the fourth century. The question remains only as to the period between that date and the issue of the autographs.

That the Traditional Text existed in that period is proved, in the absence of contemporaneous MSS. (except B and Aleph in the same century),

(1) By its undeniable prevalence afterwards. Such an almost universal prevalence implies a previous existence widely disseminated and carried down in numerous stems of descent.

(2) The verdict of contemporaneous Fathers proves this position amply.

(3) The witness of the Peshitto and Old Latin Versions confirm it, to say nothing of occasional witness to separate readings found in

the Egyptian Versions.

2. *Origin and Prevalence* of *Corruption.*

We hold that Corruption arose at the very first propagation of stories or accounts of our Lord's Life, probably even before the Gospels were written. It must have infected teaching spread from mouth to mouth, as well as writings more or less orderly, and more or less authorized. From this source mistakes must have crept in course of time, and in constant process of copying, into the authorized copies. In early though in later days as well, when or where education was not universal in the Church, and Christians had not yet imbibed familiarity with the words of Holy Scripture, Corruption spread further. A great deal of such Corruption, as we believe, found its way into the Vatican and Sinaitic manuscripts. It was persistent and multiform; and has been analyzed and explained in our second volume.[20]

3. *Dr. Hort's disagreement with us*

(1) We entirely traverse[21] the assertion, that 'no distinctly Syrian (i. e. Traditional) readings' are found amongst the earliest Fathers. Very many of the readings in the Traditional Text which are rejected by the other school are supported by those Fathers: and there is no evidence, as we maintain, to show that they pertain to the other side or to any other Text rather than to us, or that readings confessedly old and found in the Traditional Text did not belong to that Text.

---

[20] Edward Miller is speaking about the book, Vol. II, *The Causes of Corruption of the Traditional Text*, which is the companion book of *The Traditional Text of the Holy Gospels*. Both books are available from the Dean Burgon Society. (Editor, HDW)

[21] Edward Miller uses 'traverse' for 'disagree with.' (Editor, HDW)

(2) We deny the existence of any Neutral Text, except as a collection, chiefly in B and Aleph, of corrupt readings, though we admit that many of those readings, if not most of them, are of very high antiquity. Considerable danger must attend all systems founded upon Texts or Groups,—valuable as these classifications are for subsidiary employment,—because they open the way more or less to speculation and are apt to foster a shallow' and delusive sciolism[22] instead of a judicial view of evidence. Readings depending upon actual evidence afford the only true basis, though study of the causes of corruption, as well as other investigations, sheds light upon the matter.

(3) Important points of contention exist with reference to the age of the Peshitto or great Syriac Version (as to which the age of the Curetonian or Lewis is mainly a distinct question), the Theory of the Western Texts and the Latin Versions (or Version), and of Texts in general, as will be seen in the Report of the debate.

For more information, reference may be made to *The Traditional Text*, Burgon and Miller (George Bell &: Sons), 1896, and *The Causes of Corruption* (Bells), 1896. Also to Burgon's *The Revision Revised*, 1883 (John Murray), and to Miller's *Textual Guide* (Bells), 1885, and upon the question of the Peshitto, to an article in the *Church Quarterly Review* for April, 1895.

E.M.[23]

9, Bradmore Road, Oxford
May 24, 1897

---

[22] "Sciolism" means 'talking with pretended expertise.' (Editor, HDW)

[23] E.M. stands for Edward Miller. (Editor, HDW)

II.   DR. HORT'S SYSTEM

Westcott and Hort's Theory

One critic of earlier days, Griesbach by name, at the end of the last century, essayed the task of grouping, and two distinguished Cambridge scholars of our own day, Bishop Westcott and the late Professor Hort, have renewed the attempt with much greater success. They believe that by far the larger number of our extant MSS. can be shown to contain a revised (and less original) text; that a comparatively small group· has texts derived from manuscripts which escaped, or were previous to, this revision; and that, consequently, the evidence of this small group is almost always to be preferred to that of the great mass of MSS. and versions. It is this theory, which has been set out with conspicuous learning and conviction by Dr. Hort that we propose now to sketch in brief; for it appears to mark an epoch in the history of New Testament criticism.

Groups of MSS in New Testament

An examination of passages in which two or more different readings exist shows that one small group of authorities, consisting of the uncial manuscripts· B, Aleph, L, a few cursives such as Evan. 33, Act. 61, and the Memphitic and Thebaic versions, is generally found in agreement; another equally clearly marked group consists of D, the Old Latin and Old Syriac versions, and cursives 13, 69, 81 of the Gospels, 44, 137, and 180 of the Acts, and Evst. 39, with a few others more intermittently; while A, C (generally), the later uncials, and the great mass of cursives and the later versions form another group, numerically overwhelming. Sometimes each of these groups will have a distinct reading of its own; sometimes two of them will be combined against the third; sometimes an authority which usually supports one group will be found with one of the others. But the general division into groups remains constant and is the basis of the present theory.

Combined or "Conflate" Readings

Next, it is possible to distinguish the origins and relative priority of the groups. In the first place, many passages occur in which the first group described above has one reading, the second has another, and the third combines the two. Thus in the last words of St. Luke's Gospel (as the Variorum Bible shows), Aleph, B, C, L, with the Memphitic and one Syriac version, have "blessing God"; D and the Old Latin have "praising God"; but A and twelve other uncials, all the cursives, the Vulgate and other versions, have "praising and blessing God." Instances like this occur, not once nor twice, but repeatedly. Now it is in itself more probable that the combined reading in such cases is later than, and is the result of, two separate readings. It is more likely that a copyist, finding two different words in two or more manuscripts before him, would put down both in his copy, than that two scribes, finding a combined phrase in their originals, would each select one part of it alone to copy, and would each select a different one. The motive for combining would be praiseworthy—the desire to make sure of keeping the right word by retaining both; but the motive for separating would be vicious, since it involves the deliberate rejection of some words of the sacred text. Moreover we know that such combination was actually practised; for, as has been stated above, it is a marked characteristic of Lucian's edition of the Septuagint.

Localisation[24] of Groups by aid of the Fathers

At this point the evidence of the Fathers becomes important as to both the time and the place of origin of these combined (or as Dr. Hort technically calls them "conflate") readings. They are found to be characteristic of the Scripture quotations in the works of Chrysostom, who was bishop of Antioch in Syria at the end of the fourth century, and of other writers in or about Antioch at the same time; and thenceforward it is the predominant text in manuscripts, versions, and quotations. Hence this type of text, the text of our later uncials, cursives, early printed editions, and Authorised Version, is believed to have taken its rise in or near Antioch, and is known as the "Syrian" text. The type found in the second of the groups above described, that headed by D, the Old Latin and Old Syriac, is called the "Western" text, as being especially found in Latin manuscripts and in those which (like D) have both Greek and Latin texts, though it is certain that it had its origin in the East, probably in or near Asia Minor. There is another small group, earlier than the Syrian, but not represented continuously by anyone MS. (mainly by C in the Gospels, A, C, in Acts and Epistles, with certain cursives and occasionally Aleph and L), to which Dr. Hort gives the name of "Alexandrian." The remaining group, headed by B, may be best described as the "Neutral" text.

The "Syrian" Readings latest

Now among all the Fathers whose writings are left to us from before the middle of the third century (notably Irenaeus, Hippolytus, Clement, Origen, Tertullian, and Cyprian), we find readings belonging

---

[24] This is an example of the British spelling. (HDW)

to the groups described as Western, Alexandrian, and Neutral, but *no distinctly Syrian readings*.[25]   On the other hand, we have seen that in the latter part of the fourth century, especially in the region of Antioch, Syrian readings are found plentifully. Add to this the fact that, as stated above, the Syrian readings often show signs of having been derived from a combination of non-Syrian readings, and we have strong confirmation of the belief, which is the cornerstone of Dr. Hort's theory, that the Syrian type of text originated in a revision of the then existing texts, made about the end of the third century in or near Antioch. The result of accepting this conclusion obviously is, that where the Syrian text differs from that of the other groups, it must be rejected as being of later origin, and therefore less authentic; and when it is remembered that by far the greater number of our authorities contain a Syrian text, the importance of this conclusion is manifest. In spite of their numerical preponderance, the Syrian authorities must be relegated to the lowest place.

The Western Group

Of the remaining groups, the Western text is characterized by considerable freedom of addition, and sometimes of omission. Whole verses, or even longer passages, are found in manuscripts of this family, which are entirely absent from all other copies. Some of them will be found enumerated in the following chapter in the description of D, the leading manuscript of this class. It is evident that this type of text must have had its origin in a time when strict exactitude in copying the books of the New Testament was not regarded as a necessary

---

[25] The italics are Mr. Kenyon's.

virtue. In early days the copies of the New Testament books were made for immediate edification, without any idea that they would be links in a chain for the transmission of the sacred texts to a distant future; and a scribe might innocently insert in. the narrative additional details which he believed to be true and valuable. Fortunately the literary conscience of Antioch and Alexandria was more sensitive, and so this tendency did not spread very far, and was checked before it had greatly contaminated the Bible text. Western manuscripts often contain old and valuable readings, but any variety which shows traces of the characteristic Western vice of amplification or explanatory addition must be rejected, unless it has strong support outside the purely Western group of authorities.

The "Alexandrian" Group

There remain the Alexandrian and the Neutral groups. The Alexandrian text is represented, not so much by any individual MS. or version, as by certain readings found scattered about in manuscripts which elsewhere belong to one of the other groups. They are readings which have neither Western nor Syrian characteristics, and yet differ from what appears to be the earliest form of the text; and being found most regularly in the quotations of Origen, Cyril of Alexandria, and other Alexandrian Fathers, as well as in the Memphitic version, they are reasonably named Alexandrian. Their characteristics are such as might naturally be due to such a centre of Greek scholarship, since they affect the style rather than the matter, and appear to rise mainly from a desire for correctness of language. They are consequently of minor importance, and are' not always distinctly recognisable.[26]

---

[26] This is another example of the British spelling. Frequently

The "Neutral" Group

The Neutral text, which we believe to represent most nearly the original text of the New Testament, is chiefly recognisable by the absence of the various forms of aberration noticed in the other groups. Its main centre is at Alexandria, but it also appears in places widely removed from that centre. Sometimes single authorities of the Western group will part company with the rest of their family and exhibit readings which are plainly both ancient and non-Western, showing the existence of a text preceding the Western, and on which the Western variations have been grafted This text must therefore not be assigned to any local centre. It belonged originally to all the Eastern world. In many parts of the East, notably in Asia Minor, it was superseded by the text which, from its transference to the Latin churches, we call Western. It remained pure longest in Alexandria, and is fund in the writings of the Alexandrian Fathers, though even here slight changes of language were introduced, to which we have given the name of Alexandrian. Our main authority for it at the present day is the great Vatican manuscript known as B, and this is often supported by the equally ancient Sinaitic manuscript (Aleph), and by the other manuscripts and versions named above...Where the readings of this Neutral text can be plainly discerned, as by the concurrence of all or most of these authorities, they may be accepted with confidence in the face of all the numerical preponderance of other texts; and in so doing lies our best hope of recovering the true words of the New Testament.

Reference may also be made, for a short account, to the Life and Letters of Fenton John Anthony Hort, by his Son (Macmillan &

---

an "s" is placed where the Americanized spelling has a "z" (Editor, HDW).

Co.), vol. ii. Pp. 2440252; and for more information, to Dr. Hort's celebrated Introduction (Macmillan & Co.) published in 1881.

DEBATE ON TEXTUAL CRITICISM OF THE NEW TESTAMENT

THE MODERATOR: DR. INCE

DR. INCE[27]:—Gentlemen, I have accepted the invitation of Mr. Miller to preside on this occasion, coming rather as a learner. In some respects it looks as if the old custom of the Divinity Schools was being revived when there was going to be an opponent and respondent on each side, and then it was the duty of the Professor to act as moderator and sum up at the end the results of the debate. Such a moderator ought to be an expert in the subject. I cannot in the least pretend to be an expert. The exigencies of a long life in connexion with a great college which demanded so very much time, both for the tutorial work and for general superintendence, made it impossible for me to devote myself to any special research in such matters as the Textual Criticism of the Text of the Bible, even if one's own special tastes led one in that direction. Therefore that aspect of the old Divinity disputations will be wanting today. As I understand, the object of our meeting now is to hear a statement and have a discussion on the two great rival theories, as to what the true text and the original text of the

---

[27] William Ince (1825-1910) was Regius Professor of Divinity, Oxford, Fellow of Exeter College, Oxford. When the 'new' Chapel of Exeter College, Oxford was dedicated, he offered these words of wisdom: "Better to worship in the plainest barn with the full outpouring of the heart to God, than in the most gorgeous cathedral ever raised..., if only the sense of beauty finds its satisfaction there, and the heart and the life are estranged from God in Christ."

New Testament is. It is hardly necessary to say that there is a strong division of opinion between the maintainers of that which for a long time has been the received text and known as such, and the later theories of the revised text which have received exposition in the celebrated work of Bishop Westcott and Dr. Hort. Those who maintain either of these two views are to have the opportunity of expressing arguments in favour of it, and especially, I think, it is designed that Mr. Miller, who has taken an enormous amount of trouble and devoted an enormous amount of diligence and labour to the investigation of these subjects, and who stands before the world as the representative of Dean Burgon, may remove some misapprehensions which he thinks have existed in the criticisms which have been directed to the two books which he has brought out in connexion with this great question. I would only like to say that I trust the whole discussion will be conducted in a spirit of absolute judicial impartiality. **The question to be determined is, what are the scientific principles to be applied in the definition of the true text of the Bible?** (HDW, my emphasis) Many of us knew the late Dean Burgon; I knew him myself very well. Nobody could be more delighted than I was to meet him in private society, or to hear his admirable expositions in the pulpit of St. Mary's. At the same time, I must confess that the vehement tone in which he conducted some of his controversies, and his occasional imputation of motives to those who did not agree with him, rather repelled one. That was an error of a great mind, I think; and we ought to feel quite sure that an utter absence of any imputation of motives, theological or literary, should distinguish our discussion today. I have to say that it is not intended that any resolution whatever should be put; that is not really the natural sequel to such a discussion. The object is rather, I think, to direct attention, specially in Oxford, to this great question, with the hope that it will be taken up and prosecuted by scholars who have the time to devote to it, because it affects not only Greek and Syriac scholars, but all the early versions must be brought into consideration. Several gentlemen familiar with the question are going to speak, and I am instructed to call upon them in order. If the discussion should be protracted, it may be necessary to limit some of the speeches; possibly no such necessity will arise. I will begin by asking Mr. Miller to open the discussion and state his views on the subject.

Psalms 119:89 "For ever, O LORD, thy word is settled in heaven."

EDWARD MILLER'S RESPONDENT POSITION FOR DEAN BURGON

(Editor's addition of the heading, HDW)

PREBENDARY MILLER:—Dr. Ince and Gentlemen, I think that the attempt to combine scholars upon a general study of the text of Holy Scripture has been rather lost sight of during late years, although it cannot be doubted for a moment that the study is very important, and indeed the interest of it is as wide as Christendom. The system which is now in vogue—I allude of course to that of Dr. Hort—is, I find, looked upon with invincible repugnance **by a very large number of scholars**, and, speaking very briefly, I have reason to suppose that even those who hold and teach it feel some misgivings, and are not inclined to press it to the extreme extent that Dr. Hort did. (HDW, my emphasis) Turning, therefore, to the other system, which I have had the honour of presenting recently to the learned world, I wish to point out in general terms the chief characteristics of it. Dean Burgon's principles, which I advocate, have been, I think, very much misunderstood, and, as the Chairman has just said, I think there were reasons certainly of a personal character which led people to attribute undue importance to some parts of them, and generally not to understand them in their proper proportions. This, however, should be borne in mind, that Dean Burgon threw his whole intellect and powers, and devoted a very great number of years in the latter part of his life, to this work; and in order to do so, he looked at the question all round. He took the advice of some of the ablest men in the country, and then produced a system which at any rate must be said to be large-minded, even if unsound, but the large-mindedness and the soundness of it, perhaps I may be permitted to say, was, as far as I was able to judge, that which attracted myself. The chief principle of it is this, which I will state in the words of Dr. Scrivener, whose caution and care I think can hardly be doubted. He says,

> "One thing would appear at first sight almost too clear for argument, too self-evident to be disputed, that it is both our wisdom and our duty to weigh the momentous subject at issue in all its parts, shutting out from the mind no source of information which can reasonably be supposed capable of influencing our decision.'

The plain English of which is this, that Dr. Scrivener advocated a view which was supported by the large mass of MSS., against the few. He estimated the vast mass of those MSS. and other evidence which have been discovered and are known, as nineteen-twentieths, and he asks how it can be that one-twentieth shall be supposed to override the verdict of all the rest. Now it is just possible there may be some here who would like to have this exhibited in, say, two instances. Perhaps those of the rest who are familiar with them will pardon me if I bring them before the meeting. I will take first the case of the one, in the first chapter of St. Matthew, verse 25, the question of the word πρωτόκον (protokon). You remember it is rejected by some, but it is maintained in what we call the Traditional Text. With regard to the evidence for the maintenance of it, I should like to say that I do not quote Tischendorf entirely by himself. Perhaps I may be permitted to say that I am engaged in preparing a commentary which is intended to go on all the main passages considerably beyond Tischendorf, and I have finished the first ten chapters of St Matthew, from which both these instances have been taken. The evidence then is as follows:—

For the word πρωτόκον (prototokon) (firstborn), the following Uncial MSS.:—CΣDEKLMSUVΓΔΠ,—thirteen; -all collated Cursives except two; -the Old Latin MSS. f ff1 g1 q, Vulgate, Peshitto, Harkleian, Ethiopic, Armenian, Georgian, Slavonic;—Tatian, Athanasius (2.), Pseudo-Athanasius, Didymus, Cyril of Jerusalem, Basil (3), Gregory of Nyssa, Ephraem Syrus, Epiphanius (3), Chrysostom, Proclus, Isidore of Pelusium, John Damascene, Photius, Nicetas, Ambrose, Opus Imperfectum, Augustine (I believe), Jerome.

For the omission of this word we have only ℵ (the Sinaitic), B (the Vatican), Z (the Dublin Palimpsest—i. e. three Uncials;—the two Cursives (1, 33):—the Old Latin a b c g¹ k, Bohairic, Curetonian, Lewis;—of the Fathers, Ambrose (3).

Now it is quite possible that there may be more of the Fathers for this omission, which I think is very probable. Perhaps I may say that I am only beginning my work. Some weeks ago I went into the Bodleian with a number of passages, 1800, which I had taken from Dean Burgon's Indexes to the Quotations in the Fathers, to search out. These did not by any means exhaust the whole of the quotations occurring in the ten chapters, and as I have not been able to finish the investigation t cannot say whether there any more on the other side. It is very probable there are some, but I think only a few. Accordingly, this instance will illustrate what is very commonly the case, the difference between the mass of MSS on the one side and the very few on the other. My second instance is, I think, a very interesting one. We all remember Professor Huxley's paper in the Nineteenth Century about the devils going into the swine, in which he quoted St. Matthew viii. 31, as ἀπόστειλον ἡμᾶς (aposteilon êmas) (send us into the herd of swine). It is a pity that he did not prefer the reading ἐπίτρεψον ἡμῖν ἀπελθεῖν (epitrepson emin apelthein) (suffer us to go), which is much the softer of the two and takes off from the harshness of the other. But of course we must proceed upon evidence. Dean Burgon always maintained that it was not a question of opinion, but a question of actual evidence, which should rule us. Now ἐπίτρεψον ἡμῖν ἀπελθεῖν (epitrepson emin apelthein) is witnessed to by CΦ (at the end of the fifth century) EKLMSUVXΔΠ, twelve Uncials,—nearly all collated Cursives, the Old Latin f h q, Peshitto, Harkleian,— whilst Σ (at the beginning of the ninth century) reads ἐπίτρεψον ἡμῖν εἰσελθεῖν (epitrepson emin eiselthein), which is practically the same, and the variations of one Cursive which reads ἡμας and of six which omit ἡμῖν altogether, do not prevent them from being reckoned as supporters of the rest. On the other hand, for ἀπόστειλον ἡμας only two Uncial MSS., B ℵ, can be reckoned,—only four Cursives (to follow Tischendorf, for my work here is not complete), 1, 22, 33, 118,-with the Versions a b c d ff¹ g¹ kl, Vulgate, Bohairic, Sahidic, Ethiopic, Arabic.

That will show, what will be perfectly familiar to those who have looked thoroughly into these questions, the extreme difference there is between the two contentions. The remarkable thing is, that that extreme difference is kept up to a very great extent indeed throughout the Gospels. In almost all controverted cases you will find, and this is a misfortune, Aleph and B or one of them, with a very small body on one side and a large body of other MSS on the other. I say that is a misfortune, because I think it is that which divides us into two camps, a thing I very much regret. This being so, if you have a very small body of MSS against all the others, how can it possibly be right to say that the small body should dominate all the rest? Just look at the matter for an instant in this way: Suppose you are sitting at the elbow of an editor of Agamemnon, or the Trachiniae, or whatever it may be of

Sophocles, you would see that in his very wildest dreams he would never conceive on any difficult passage of such an immense mass of evidence being at hand, as we have in this case on the one side set aside by those few. And yet when one looks at Dr. Hort's system, one finds a large body of evidence frequently thrown entirely aside and virtually cast into the waste-paper basket. I will ask, is that a logical or a proper way of proceeding? Can it be justified intellectually, and can it be right, in dealing with Holy Scripture? The explanation is what has frequently been called by other men the extreme adulation paid to B, especially by Dr. Hort and men of that side. I think some of it is very natural, and that history quite accounts for it. They are the two oldest MSS; and in early times, when people had in their view only a small amount of evidence, it was very natural that they should say that these two MSS which come to us as the earliest, and were therefore nearest to the original autographs, should be right. A great deal of interest was also felt because 'B' in the Vatican was invested with a certain amount of mystery. People were in the habit of looking for great things to come from Rome, and being unable to learn what it was which was so zealously guarded, they thought it would prove to be the key to all the difficulties when it was discovered. . Thus, when another MS like Aleph was found by Tischendorf, it was only reasonable that great attention should be paid to it.

Yet when we look on the other side, there are certain points which cast discredit upon those two documents. In the first place, according to all the critics they were produced in those times after the Council of Nicea when Semi-Arianism or one of those kinds of belief which were associated with it were in the ascendant; and it was very remarkable that just at the time when the Nicene Creed was finally accepted, towards the end of the century, these MSS seem to have slipped out of repute. Then also they bear I think upon them traces of a somewhat sceptical[28] tone, sometimes almost going into heresy, which would enable one, as I think, to connect them with the period in which they were produced. They are too incomplete MSS. There are no breathings or accents and scarcely any stops in B, and there are no breathings or accents except in two passages in Aleph and the stops are very fitful and uncertain. These MSS were also, as I have pointed out, condemned within fifty years. There was, I think, a great deal involved in that circumstance. And lastly, they are rejected by evidence virtually older than themselves. Objection was made to Dean Burgon that he did not care for the value of MSS. This is quite untrue as far as feelings were concerned, although of course you must not simply depend upon what a man's feelings are to maintain anything respecting his actions.

But Dean Burgon did not neglect the special value of separate MSS. At least it will be admitted that he entertained and expressed very strong objection, in which many others concurred, to the very high estimate formed by many critics of B and Aleph. If there is on one side a very high admiration for these MSS, there is also on the other side a large number of scholars who have a great objection to them. There are many eminent men on our side, and I think if you set store by the admiration for Aleph and B on the one side you ought to put the objections to them in the other scale. It was said that Dean Burgon merely counted heads, and that the character or weight of MSS was therefore virtually nothing, it being supposed that he imagined one to be equal to another. But Dean Burgon never adopted this line of argument. Some people are of opinion that he thought a late Cursive was as good as an early Uncial, but this was not the case, and he and those who agree with him have never dreamt of maintaining such a

---

[28] British spelling. (HDW)

thesis. What we have always said is, that when the mass of the later MSS go together they outweigh one or two other ones. We never take the Cursives separately.

In order to controvert the erroneous impression regarding his views that he cared for numbers only and not for weight, Dean Burgon constructed and worked out to a considerable extent his theory about the seven notes of truth, which he maintained were:—Antiquity, number, variety of kinds and countries, weight, continuity, context, and internal evidence. He laid great stress upon antiquity. Of course number is something, for if you multiply evidence by any figure it is surely of more value when it is numerous than when it was single, although one would be almost inclined to suppose that some people imagine that number derogates from the value.

There is no time now to dwell upon the remaining notes of truth. But there is one other point which I should like to notice before I go further, and that is this. There are three classes of evidence:—Greek MSS, Versions into different languages, and Quotations of the New Testament by the Fathers. Some people suppose that we lay more stress upon the Quotations of the Fathers than upon anything else. That is quite an error; we lay most stress upon MSS and anybody who goes carefully into the evidence and into the different passages must I think do the same. Suppose we come to a passage which is not a very important one perhaps, and which is perfectly decided by the copies, we say that there is no necessity to go further and to call in the Versions and the Fathers. The MSS themselves decide the question, and great care ought to be exercised in applying the other two classes of evidence. I think on some occasions Tischendorf has wrongly quoted Latin MSS when there is not sufficient evidence to justify such a course, the difference of reading being capable of explanation by the difference of idiom and not necessarily by any question connected with special words. And then again with regard to the Fathers, it is evident that great caution must be employed in dealing with them. You must be cautious how far they are used, but in many respects they are most valuable, especially perhaps in regard to such matters as omissions. For instance in the case, say, of the word πρωτότοκον (prototokon) (where the mention shows that it was in the Fathers' copy), or especially when a reference is made not in exact quotation but as an explanation of a passage—then the Fathers become extremely valuable. Another caution is to be urged with respect to Texts of the Fathers, some scholars holding the objection that the words may have been altered. My impression is that if those Texts were looked through thoroughly, these critics would withdraw a great part of their objection. Of course, we wait for the editing of the Fathers, but if we take editions like Stieren's Irenaeus, or Otto's Justin Martyr, we find the changes are very few and small. The principle I venture to lay down therefore is that of the many against the few, and the necessity for a careful consideration and weighing of the evidence.

Passing from that, I want to draw your attention to another point upon which there has been some misapprehension, and that is the claim we make for the acceptance of fifteen centuries impressed upon the Traditional Text. People have thought when we spoke of the Church doing this, that we had in our minds some arbitrary decision to which all people were bound to pay attention. Instead of that, we urge it as a proof of reasonableness. It is well known by those who study the history of the Church, that even the clear and plain decisions of Councils were not taken to be final or to have the authority of General Councils until they were subsequently ratified by the Universal Church. They were examined on all sides, and when they were approved, respect gathered round the Council in question, and the decisions of it became valid and fixed. There was, of course, in the present case, no public controversy; so far as we know, any such must have been between man and man, and not, at any rate, so public as to descend to us. That I think renders the decision even more strong. Then I wish to remind you that the period to which we refer was the fourth century, which was the great verifying age of the Church. Soon after the time when the Roman Empire became Christian, all the finest intellects in the world were turned towards these subjects, upon which people felt and thought more than upon anything else. As an illustration of this, I may refer you to the great respect paid today to the Nicene Creed, or again the respect felt for the Canon of Holy Scripture. When they had decided upon the Canon of the New Testament, surely they must go on to settle the words of the New Testament, and they so seem to have done. But this became a much longer process, because there were but a few books upon each of which the Canon would have to be settled, but innumerable readings. Accordingly, a long period of years would be taken up in the settlement of the vast numbers of questions involved. The fortunes of the Roman Empire delayed it very much, and the consequence is that the final settlement has not been made, as we maintain, up to the present time, when our immense collection of evidence puts us in a much better position to form our conclusions than at any previous time. The process of settlement went on until the end of the seventh century, and in saying this I have the agreement also of Dr. Hort. After that time the Traditional Text, which had been mainly received before, was finally settled and accepted. The fact that this was the great verifying age of the Church did not mean that there were any new decisions made:—they made no fresh departure, but they simply ratified what had been in practice in the Church before. This ratification was expressed in the words uttered at the Council of Nicea by all the bishops, τὰ ἀπχαῖα ἔθη κπατείτω, 'Let ancient customs prevail.' Therefore when the question of the Text was settled, it is reasonable to suppose that it was decided that the Traditional Text was the Text which had been mainly read and used from very earliest times, and that it was a part of ancient custom. So that leads us, I think, to see that in Dr. Hort's system, and in other systems before his, there was a narrow view of estimating tradition. I think the authors did not see the vast volume of tradition which descended all over the Church, but were inclined to trace everything through a small body, such as the school at Caesarea.[29] I think we hardly understand the extraordinary attention paid to Holy Scriptures in the earliest times. It is very remarkable that many more quotations were found from the Old Testament in the works of the early Fathers, than from the New. And the reason is clear. People outside the Church first had to understand the nature of the One True God, and then to come to Him. They learnt that in the Old Testament, and that was what struck them more than all, and when they had been taught that, they could go on to the teaching of the New. In this way the Holy Scriptures, Old and New, were a most powerful engine, first of all in the conversion of the people and then in teaching them; and so for their own study they must have had copies all over the Church. They read them also in their services, and wherever there was a church there must have been MSS of Holy Scriptures in daily use. When one decayed, it was replaced by another. So there was not a

---

[29] The school of Caesarea was established by Origen after he was run out of Alexandria. The library was established by his student, Pamphilus, who became the instructor and close friend of Eusebius, the Bishop of Caesarea. Eusebius was Emperor Constantine's theologian. He was tapped by the Emperor to provide 25 copies of the Bible for the Roman Empire. Evidence strongly suggests he used Origen's material from the Hexapla. (Editor's footnote, HDW)

country where there was not some stream or streams of descent, like the Western Text and the Alexandrian. I quite agree that those texts existed; but besides them there was not a place that did not hand on the tradition, which was carried down as if in rivulets extending over the whole surface of the Church. If this was the case, it shows the reason why two MSS of the same text, issuing probably from the school at Caesarea, should not have been accepted all over the Church. There was an immense volume of tradition at variance with them, and that was the reason why their text fell out of general vogue within fifty years after those MSS were made.

You require some proof. I think I have some as far as it goes. You remember that some 'of the chief men who established the Nicene Creed finally in universal acceptance were St. Basil and the two St. Gregories. It is remarkable that these three Fathers witness very largely, more than almost any others of their time, to the Traditional Text, or rather the traditional readings, and you will remember that all these three came from Cappadocia, two from Neo-Caesarea, and one of the Gregories from Nazianzus, not very far from Caesarea. Does not that seem to show there was a descent genealogically of MSS in favour of the Traditional Text which taught them to witness so much to it? There is even a little more proof that such a tradition was carried on in those parts. In the early centuries Gregory Thaumaturgus, a pupil of Origen, witnessed to the Traditional Text just about in the same way, and he also lived at Neo-Caesarea.

This brings us back to the very difficult time before we have any MSS existing which reaches back to the delivery of the autographs. With respect to that you will remember, in the first place, that it is now generally understood that the reason why we have no MSS is, because the New Testament was in early days written upon papyrus, which was of a perishable character, and therefore they have not descended to us. Many of you will remember that last year, by the kindness of the Margaret Professor, we had in a lecture given by Mr. Kenyon some specimens of papyrus shown us; and, as a matter of fact, he went rather farther than I am myself disposed to go. But there is no doubt, I fancy, that in the first days they used papyrus, and that is the reason why we have no MSS in our hands representing those times. Before I go into that subject I think there is a point which is very much deserving of consideration, and I find that it has not only struck myself, but it has struck at any rate one of my learned friends. It is that Dr. Hort has strained the theory of Texts, and that generally among critics the theory of Texts has been strained in its consideration. I am not going to say anything against the theory of Texts generally within due limitations. It was introduced by Bengel, who was followed by Semler and Griesbach and Hug, and it was adopted in this century by others, and especially by Dr. Hort. He slightly altered it by the introduction of what he called the Neutral Text. He considered that in the early times there were three texts: the Western, the Alexandrian, and the Neutral. I should say we doubt very much indeed the existence of the Neutral Text, except in a very particular way which I will describe directly, and upon which I maintain that the evidence is satisfactorily strong. When people read about a Text they are apt to consider that it must be some complete setting of words and expressions. And indeed, what is said and written about it sometimes leads me to suppose that they consider everything written in the West belonged to the Western Text, whereas of course Text is merely a collective word denoting a number of readings in the particular part of the world to which it refers. Besides these, it includes also other readings which belong to the true Text, whatever that may be. In early times people took the general readings of the New Testament and added some peculiar ones of their own which prevailed especially in the locality, and that was the way in which they made a composite kind of Text, partly belonging to the true Text, and partly coloured with readings of their own. Now what we ought to call them is, I maintain, not Texts but Readings. When you once begin to speak of Texts, and consequently a beginner comes to consider Texts, he naturally clothes the word so to speak with flesh and bones and makes it into something; whereas if it is merely collective, it is a very different matter. This, I maintain, is the only way of safeguarding them, viz., to call them Readings instead of Texts. It comes to this. Supposing we were to take in the early days a map of the Church, instead of having red or whatever colour it may be in the West, and yellow for Alexandria and so forth, we should dot the world all over. There were everywhere reasons for corruption which must have been produced in early times. It was so produced all about the Christian world, but in certain particular regions you would have more marks, as I maintain, of corruption, and perhaps also slightly different in characteristics. I think that is a very important point, and must lead, if it is not attended to, to mistakes. *Dolus latet sub verbo* Text.

There are also difficulties in this way. Alexandrian is a very perplexing Text to make out, and with respect to the Western there is a very considerable difficulty there too, because the Old Latin Versions differ so very much among themselves. Beginning with the Brixianus (f) on the one hand and ending with the Bobiensis (k) there is an immense amount of variety, so that on very many passages you are able to use on both sides Old Latin Texts. I think it is much safer to follow to a great extent Dean Burgon' theory, which is worked out very ingeniously upon the various Kinds of Corruption.

With respect to the origin of B and Aleph, which will be of

course Neutral documents, I believe both came from Origen, who was the first textual critic. I think Dean Burgon has been hard upon him sometimes. He (Origen, HDW) was a man of wide observation, and had travelled very largely. He went to Rome, besides living at Alexandria, to Arabia Petraea thrice, to Caesarea several times, besides spending there the latter part of his life. He also went to Greece, and sojourned in Neo-Caesarea. As you know, he edited the Old Testament, and prepared an apparatus of MSS for editing the New. He can frequently be quoted on both sides, for he used MSS of a different character; and it seems therefore that he laid his foundations as widely as he could with a view to a future revision or settlement of the Text. Moving from Alexandria he went to live at Caesarea, where he laid the foundation of the school at that place, in which he was followed by those who were successively bishops of that city, Pamphilus, Eusebius, Acacius, and Euzoius. The two latter were engaged, as we are told in a colophon, in copying from papyrus on to vellum. There are various reasons for concluding, and I think it is generally admitted now, that the probability is, at least as far as the evidence goes, that the fifty MSS. produced by Eusebius in compliance with the letter from Constantine included the Sinaitic and the Vatican. Now taking into consideration these fifty MSS., seeing there were forty-eight others, my impression is, that they were according to the school of Origen of different characters. Supposing they were not, but that, as Dr. Hort might say, all the fifty were B's and Alephs, how would he explain this? They went to Constantinople, and were used in the Churches there. Supposing they embodied in them the true Text, they must have had an almost untold influence. They came from the highest school, were exceedingly handsome, and if they all agreed must have impressed their character upon the Church at Constantinople. Yet so soon was the Traditional

Text accepted at Constantinople, that those in the last century who treated of the earliest Texts styled that . Text Constantinopolitan or Byzantine, which Dr. Hort calls Syrian, and which we call the Traditional. How then can this be explained? I conclude therefore that these MSS. were not of the same, but of various kinds.

I have very little more time, and I must very rapidly say what I have to say. The evidence in the early centuries is this. It is **first** of the MSS, because the Traditional Text from the later part of the fourth century prevailed almost everywhere, and there were after that time hardly any of the others. Supposing it was general, almost universal, everywhere found to prevail, it must have been the successor of copies of the same character which went before it. Therefore the MSS throw back their character to the earliest age. **Secondly**, there is the evidence of the Fathers, which I have in our first volume gone through and have shown that by a very large majority they witness to the Traditional Text. With respect to this subject I must point out that those who maintain B and Aleph have a very much more difficult task to perform than we have. We admit that readings of their character go back to the first, but we call them corruptions. We admit they were quite as early and came out immediately after—perhaps even before— the Gospels were written; but our opponents say that our readings do not go back at all. Therefore we have simply to prove that our readings go back to that time, in order to show that those who are opposed to us are wrong in giving a late date to the Traditional Text. Then, **thirdly**, there are the Versions, and of those first comes the Peshitto. With respect to the controversy about the Peshitto, whether that or the Curetonian was the old Syriac Version or not, a great deal of evidence will be given to you by those who have expressly studied the subject. One point I notice which has for me a good deal of interest. By the end of the sixth century the apparatus of MSS of the Peshitto exceeded the apparatus of the Greek MSS of the Gospels. Does not that show how very firmly the Peshitto must have been settled? What is settled in the unchangeable East goes on; and accordingly that seems to be a strong argument, as well as the others, in favour of the early existence of the Peshitto. Next I take the question relating to the revision of the Traditional Text. The Latin Versions, according to my figures, witness in favour of the Traditional Text in the proportion of five to four. You will see here the exclusiveness of Dr. Hort, and I venture to hope the greater broadness of our school.

There is one point which perhaps I may be allowed to enter upon before I end. It is this. Dr. Hort's system stands of course in our way, and I think there are very great objections to it. The first perhaps that one might notice, which is felt by many people very strongly, is that in order to support it he is obliged to suppose that certain revisions took place of which there is no trace whatever in history. I do not wish to dilate upon that now; but I know there are some, and perhaps several here, who feel that that is a very strong point. Possibly I may mention a little private instance of this. A few years ago at Bournemouth a friend of mine introduced me to the late Dr. Scott, Head Master of Westminster School, who divided the honours at Cambridge in his year with the present distinguished Bishop of Durham. He said, 'If you get Scott upon the "phantom revisions," as we call them, it will delight your soul.' He called upon me: and I introduced the subject. It was like turning on a tap; he was thoroughly indignant at the liberty taken with history by Dr. Hort. I only mention this to show you what is thought by very able men, who are quite capable of judging of history, if they are not actually experts upon this subject.

There is another point, that of Conflation: I want particularly to mention this. It has been said in the Life of Dr. Hort, that he would not reply to Dean Burgon because he thought that Dean Burgon did not know enough to grapple with and estimate his Inductive Theory. I have my doubts, but I will not say anything about whether Dean Burgon had not examined more Greek MSS. and had a greater command of Patristic quotations than Dr. Hort; our contention is that Dr. Hort's theory is an Inductive Theory without induction. As a matter of fact, there has been no inductive foundation published. It now remains in pigeon-holes or MS books, and the world has not seen it. But I also hold, that it is not supported by any induction adequate to the maintenance of it. Now conflation supplies a field small enough to test this in. Dr. Hort—I speak very briefly (having no time to pay tribute to his many admirable qualities)—only brings forward eight instances,—unless perhaps there is one more mentioned just on his way,—eight instances to establish a system which is supposed to operate throughout the whole of the Gospels. I say that that is an absurd induction, but I have answered his eight pleas, and in the opinion of one of my critics have had the best of the argument. That however may pass. Eight instances—four from St. Mark, four from St. Luke, none from St. Matthew unless it is the one I have just noticed, and none from St. John! Yet St. John especially is just the writer whom you would have thought would have supplied several such, his writings being quite of the character required. I say that this is an absurd foundation upon which to build up a large doctrine. I tried my best to increase Dr. Hort's number, and I added twenty-four to it, so as to make eight for each Gospel. All these but one answered the conditions at first, but failed in meeting the requirements afterwards. It is quite possible that I have made a mistake, and have been unable to discover what really exists. I am quite prepared to suppose that there may be several. A friend of mine showed me seven which he had found out, where curiously enough, whilst five of the conflations were towards the Traditional Text, the others were towards B or Aleph, and therefore in the wrong direction. In order to satisfy the conditions of this problem, it would be necessary to have at least thirty instances, and these should be typical instances. I give a challenge here to the followers of Dr. Hort either to produce thirty typical instances or to reject the system altogether.

Just in conclusion, let me say that although in principle there can be no compromise between idolatry of B and Aleph and an adherence to a broad view of evidence, nevertheless, although no theoretical compromise is possible, I should hope that there may be a practical meeting in many ways: and what I should hope very much is, that some plan may be set on foot from this time by which those who are on different sides on this question may find some sort of agreement and may co-operate one with another in threshing out this great question. It is with that wish that I have done what I could in this debate, proposed to me kindly by the Margaret Professor. I have to thank you all for the attention you have given me, and I only hope some good result may come of our meeting together today.

WILLIAM SANDAY'S

OPPONENT POSITION

AGAINST DEAN BURGON

(Editor's addition of the heading, IIDW)

PROFESSOR SANDAY:-I very gladly acknowledge, and I am sure every one here will acknowledge, the chivalrous spirit in which Mr. Miller has prosecuted this controversy, and the chivalrous character of the proposals which he has made to us; I refer in particular to those for co-operation. But I think that there will be practical difficulties in the way of carrying out these suggestions to any large extent. I think it would be better for each side to prosecute its own studies on its own methods, but I do not see any reason whatever why we should not meet from time to time in a friendly way as we have done this afternoon, and discuss particular points, perhaps somewhat more limited in character than the very broad issue which is put before us to-day. I must try to be as concise as possible, and I will begin by meeting Mr. Miller as far as I can by saying how far I think we can go - with him. I think we can go with him **first** as to the palaeographical conditions of textual criticism. It happens that that side of the subject is one to which I have paid a good deal of attention from time to time myself, and I very gladly bear testimony to what Mr. Miller has said in his books on this subject. He carries me entirely with him as to, for instance, the point he mentions regarding the supersession of papyrus by vellum. This was an important epoch in the history of MSS. There are a number of other points into which I need not at present enter.

The **second** point upon which I agree with him is the general enumeration of the causes of corruption. I willingly recognize all the causes that he mentions in his book which goes under that title. The only question is as to their application. Unfortunately, this is practically a question of internal evidence, and this internal evidence is constantly ambiguous. One reading may be due to one kind of corruption, and an opposite reading may be due to another kind of corruption, so that the one very often cancels the other. The difference between us is not as to the causes of corruption which are in operation, but as to the application of those causes. **Thirdly**, there is a point in his books on which Mr. Miller has laid some stress, and that is the influence of the great libraries. There again I agree with him, and in particular regarding that one great library upon which one naturally has one's eye—I mean the library founded by Pamphilus at Caesarea. The reference to this would be specially important if it were true, as Mr. Miller and many others contend, that the great MSS., the Vatican and the Sinaitic, both came from that library. I confess I think myself that there is a great deal to be said for that view. But it is not quite proved. Dr. Hort thought, they were written in Italy, or rather that the Vatican MS. was written in Italy and the Sinaitic probably in Egypt. There are some arguments to be adduced in favour of this view. There is a little peculiarity found in B which is characteristic of the Latin MSS—a tendency to represent the form 'Israel' by 'Istrael,' the insertion of a 't.' It is confined to the Acts in B, and there are certain capitulations or chapters, marked in the margin, which are also found in a Latin form. These are, of course, arguments, and we must remember that the great palaeographer,[30] Dr. Ceriani of Milan, was also of opinion that B was written in Italy. There is a great deal to be

---

[30] British spelling. (HDW)

said on the other side; the question is still under discussion. Then, **fourthly**, I can for myself go with Mr. Miller to a certain extent in thinking that Dr. Westcott and Dr. Hort have pressed their preference for these MSS rather too far. One can make that confession without any breach of principle, without any real inconsistency, because there are other texts almost, if not quite, as early as they are. The Western text and those texts represented by these two MSS branched off in the second century, and so the true reading may be found in either of those two branches, and occasionally I think it quite possible—as indeed Westcott and Hort themselves thought in the case of certain omissions in the Western authorities—that the right reading may be preserved in the Western branch and not in the branch represented by Aleph and B. After all, they are fallible MSS. You find, but only very occasionally, the same kind of mistakes as in other MSS; and it is, I think, not a safe inference that because a MS is right in nine cases out of ten, therefore it will be right in the tenth. On this fourth point I can agree with Mr. Miller; but I am afraid, on the other hand, there is a fundamental difference between us, and that difference is so grave that it would not be easy for us actually to work together at present. We start from opposite ends. Mr. Miller and Dean Burgon started from the Received Text, and I cannot help thinking that the Received Text has so impressed itself upon their minds that it is the standard to which, unconsciously, everything is referred. One can see it in their books; one almost seems to read the Received Text between the lines. That is one thing, and the other thing is, I think, that one can also read between the lines that strong preference which Mr. Miller has expressed for numbers, for the numerical majority, the mass of MSS. Whether this view is correct is exceedingly doubtful, but one cannot be surprised at finding it advocated. The other view seems a paradox, but it is much less of a paradox than it seems. Take this simple illustration. Suppose you have a MS. from which, from time to time, fifty copies are made. On Mr. Miller's theory those fifty copies would entirely outweigh the MS itself, whereas all of them would contain such corruptions as are to be found in the original MS, and each of them would have its own corruptions as well. Clearly, the single MS is of more value than the whole fifty. That is the principle upon which we go, and I submit, with all deference, that Mr. Miller presents the problem in a wrong way. The real problem is to get at the original archetype, to get as near the autograph as you possibly can. MSS fall into groups or families, each of which has an archetype. You begin with small families, and try to find what were the readings contained in this small archetype. A group of small families will make a large family, which also has its archetype. The true method of criticism is to work your way backwards, starting from the outside and working your way gradually to the root. I submit that that is the right method of approaching the subject. Another thing which I am glad to see in Mr. Miller's recent book is the prominence which he has given to the history of the text. Hitherto, in Dean Burgon's earlier works that side of the question was certainly not prominently put forward. But Dr. Hort lays it down as a principle that in order to get at the original text you must first have some conception of its history. That is a perfectly sound principle, not confined to the New Testament, but applicable to any text, for which there are a great number of excellent authorities. Of course, if you have only a single MS, and if you have a MS. from which others are copied, as in the case of Sophocles, the problem is a perfectly simple one. The text practically has no history, at least it is only guess-work to decide regarding it. But where you have so many authorities as we have for the Greek Testament, it is possible to a very considerable extent to reconstruct that history. That was the problem which Dr. Westcott and Dr. Hort set before themselves, and worked out with extraordinary skill and patience. And perhaps I may be allowed to say that my own experience, so far as it goes, very much confirms their results. To a certain extent that experience is independent, because I was working on the subject of text before their book came out. The first-fruits of such work as I did upon the subject may be seen in my book on the *Gospels in the Second Century*, and I have by me at home numbers of tables which I drew out for myself at that time. They were constructed on the principle of beginning with what was easy, and going from easy readings to difficult ones. This is another mistake which it seems to me has been made by the supporters of the Received Text. They pick out the salient points, and give you all the striking readings. You are not led up to those readings, you are led down to them from the Received Text, and I confess I think that the other method is preferable. When you have examined a number of easy readings you will find principles will gradually form themselves in your mind. Of course I have learnt more than I can say from Westcott and Hort, and I should be only too glad to be allowed to consider myself one of their disciples. But now in view of Mr. Miller's recent books I think we may say that we have two theories of the history of the text confronting each other, this theory of Dr. Hort, and that presented by Mr. Miller. Well, I confess that for myself I have no doubt as to which deserves the preference. Mr. Miller will forgive me if I say that history as it is presented by him makes upon me the impression of an afterthought, whereas in the case of Dr. Hort it was the very foundation of the whole system. He had to work out the history as an essential and integral part of the theory. I must just say a few words in reply to the points raised by Mr. Miller, and in support of that general view. Mr. Miller objects to Dr. Hort's use of the term

'Texts.' I quite agree with him that it is only a collective name for a number of readings, but it does correspond to certain facts, certain phenomena in the MSS. There is a tendency for MSS and for other authorities to form into groups, and when you come to examine the readings of those groups you find certain common characteristics running through them. That is all that it means. You may sit lightly to them, especially in the matter of geography, as Mr. Miller pointed out. That is one point. Then I understand that Mr. Miller now lays stress on the authority of the Church from the end of the fourth century onwards. I am not sure that I know exactly what he means. Does he think there was an authorized edition? If so, it seems to me hardly consistent with his criticism of what he calls the 'phantom revisions,' because there is no trace of any such authoritative revision. On the contrary, I should say you find writers of that age occasionally referring to differences of reading, and referring to them in the same way that they had done before. They do not appeal to authority. You may occasionally find the statement that the Church reads so and so; you may find that the ecclesiastical copies have such and such a reading, but more often you find the statement that the ancient copies read so and so. I should like to give Mr. Miller one example. There is a conspicuous reading in which St. Basil who was one of the persons mentioned as supporting this authoritative text—

MR. MILLER:-Yes, perhaps I may explain. I meant merely the action going through the Church.

PROFESSOR SANDAY:—You mean a gradual tendency?

MR. MILLER:—I quite agree. I think it merely grew up, so to speak. I ought to have guarded myself.

PROFESSOR SANDAY:—I think you will find, when you come to examine the matter, that Dr. Hort did not mean anything more. I was just going to quote this particular reading of St. Basil. I quite allow that St. Basil has a good many readings which correspond with the Received Text, but he also has a fair proportion of others, and you remember the reading of the first verse of the Epistle to the Ephesians, in which there is an omission of the words ἐν ᾽Εφέσῳ (en Epheso). The authorities for that omission are Aleph and B, alone among the MSS, Origen and Basil, the latter of whom also quotes ancient MSS. If you take St. Jerome you will find the same appeal to MSS, and in particular to the MSS of Origen, *Codices Adamantii et Pierii*. There is a special appeal made to them. I am afraid that the view will not hold water that Aleph and B represent the text of Origen. The text they really represent is older than Origen, because there are a great many examples of readings which Origen advocates strongly, but which are not to be found in Aleph and B. Origen reads 'Bethabara beyond Jordan;' Aleph and B have 'Bethany.' In the case of the miracle of the demoniac Origen reads 'Gergesenes,' and defends the reading at considerable length, whereas Aleph and B have Gadarenes.' It is true there is a large element of Aleph and B which is attested by Origen. Then it is true there is a tendency for the Text which is ultimately represented in the Received Text, for the Traditional Text as it is called, to gain ground in the latter part of the fourth century, and you would no doubt find it to a considerable extent in Gregory Nazianzen and Gregory of Nyssa. Of course, according to Dr. Hort, the home of this Text really is Antioch, whence it spread. The way in which Dr. Hort accounts for its prevalence in later ages is not by the fact that it was regarded as in any way authoritative, but simply because of the great influence which Antioch exercised upon Constantinople at the end of the century. You have St. Chrysostom transferred from Antioch to Constantinople as Patriarch, and there are a good many other points tending in the same direction. Its prevalence, therefore, is accounted for partly in that way, and partly also by the fact that the Church very soon afterwards lost its other great provinces. You have the wave of the Mahommedan invasion in the seventh century. First Syria and Palestine were lost, and then Egypt and Africa. Almost all the Christian provinces were blotted out from the map, not entirely or absolutely, but still to a very large extent. Constantinople became the centre of the Christian world, and the Text which prevailed there prevailed all over the Greek-speaking world, because by that time, you will see, the West was purely Latin, and Constantinople was I have no doubt a great centre for the manufacture of MSS. That is the way in which Dr. Hort would account for this set of facts. To the prevalence of the Antiochene Text towards the end of the century there are very large and important exceptions. The greatest critic of the age, St. Jerome, does not take that Text. Mr. White and Bishop Wordsworth have been investigating the character of the Greek MSS used by St. Jerome in his revision of the Greek Testament. I will not anticipate Mr. White's answer to this question, but I do not think you will find it is Antiochene. Then also I think it would be wrong to identify this Text with the cause of orthodoxy. What greater champion of orthodoxy have you than St. Cyril of Alexandria, and yet you will find he very frequently sides with the two condemned MSS, Aleph and B. Mr. Miller will, perhaps, rather allow me to question that point among the accusations he brought against those two MSS. The number of readings which might be supposed to have any taint of scepticism or heresy about them is exceedingly small in these two MSS. They extend over the whole of the New Testament, and readings which have that kind of tendency are very few. To set against them you have very striking examples which tell exactly the other way; for instance, the great reading, μονογενης Θεός (monogenes Theos), in the first chapter of John. Perhaps some day Mr. Miller will collect and print a few examples, because, although he refers to them in his book, he quotes exceedingly few, and they are not really heresy, as heresy goes. Then, just to bring things to an issue, as I say,' Mr. Miller offers us a reconstruction of the history of the Text, and Dr. Hort offers the same. I admit that it is very largely hypothetical; but if Dr. Hort's view is correct, there is no evidence at all of the existence of the particular kind of Text which Mr. Miller prefers further back than the latter part of the third or the beginning of the fourth century. That is his contention—I know Mr. Miller would not allow it for a moment—but he quotes examples of earlier readings, of traditional readings, which are supported by earlier authorities. All that is perfectly allowed for in Dr. Hort's theory. His theory is simply based upon the phenomena of MSS. You have three groups of authorities supporting characteristic readings. There is a group represented by Aleph and B, a group commonly known as the Western Text, represented by Latin authorities, and primarily also by Syriac authorities. There is no question at all that this group is an exceedingly early one; in any case it goes back to the second century. You will find readings of that character in writers of the second and third centuries in great abundance. There is also a smaller group, more difficult to distinguish, and yet which is a substantial group, of what are called Alexandrian readings. There is no question that these types of Text were all current in the second and third centuries; but when you come to look for characteristic readings of what is called the Traditional Text, you do not find them before the fourth century, and Dr. Hort's theory is that that Text was an eclectic Text, produced by a comparison between and a combination of those previously existing Texts. So if you get a traditional reading supported by early authorities, early MSS, early

Fathers, and so on, Dr. Hort would say at once, 'That is a Western reading adopted in the Traditional Text.' There are a great many Western readings which are not adopted, but a certain proportion of them are. So that what I say is, that it is all allowed for; you may be quite sure that all these phenomena are allowed for in Dr. Hort's theory. And when I have said that my own experience went to confirm that, all I mean is this: not that there are not a great number of open questions and many doubtful readings, in regard to which it is difficult to make up one's mind, but one has very little difficulty indeed in putting all the phenomena which come before one into their place in the theory. Thus the Lewis MS, which was discovered the other day, and which is of extreme importance, takes its place at once in the scheme of Texts, and its discovery would not have affected Dr. Hort's conclusions, except to a very infinitesimal degree, because it had all been allowed for beforehand. I am afraid I must say that Mr. Miller's presentation of the history of Texts is not one which we can accept just as it stands. Those readings require a great deal of scrutiny; it is a delicate and a difficult matter to decide regarding them, especially the further back you go.

An instance has just come before me. I have had occasion to work at Hilary, who is one of the authorities for reading ὁ μονογενής (ho monogenes) in St. John 1:18. It is perfectly true he quotes the passage two or three times, and always in that way, and no doubt that was the reading of the Western MS. But repeatedly—you may count the examples by the score—he has that remarkable phrase *Unigenitus Deus*. One reading he got from the Latin MSS, and the other from some other source; probably during his travels in the East he may have heard it pass from mouth to mouth. There is one question Mr. Miller has raised which is of considerable importance, viz. the character of the

Peshitto, which is the sheet anchor of Mr. Miller's theory. It is the oldest text in any case which is of that particular type. So you see it is a question of considerable importance when this version was made. Was it made towards the end of the third century, or was it made in the second? No doubt it is an argument, and an argument of considerable weight, which impresses the imagination, to quote the fact that there were so many MSS of the Peshitto in existence as early as the sixth century, and even one or two I think in the fifth century. Still this is not supported by the evidence of ecclesiastical writers, and in any case there is no proof that the Peshitto goes back to anything like the second century. I have only two other short points with which to deal. One is the question of conflation. Mr. Miller threw out a challenge to the followers of Dr. Hort to produce at least thirty typical instances of his theory of conflation. I think the number is a very good estimate; I do not suppose there are many more than thirty. I am speaking at a guess. I dare say there may not be more than that number; but what of that? If Mr. Miller will allow me to say so, he did not represent Dr. Hort quite justly when he said this was a phenomenon running all through the Gospels. Dr. Hort would not profess that it ran all through the Gospels. What he says is that occasionally you do find these combined readings—a double reading, representing, say, one the Western Text and the other the reading of Aleph and B, or what might be called the Alexandrian reading. It is not by any means a constant phenomenon. Whatever person or whatever school produced the Traditional Text, did not systematically combine the Texts. They were combined occasionally, and that is all one can say. Also I am prepared to admit for myself that the conflations are not conclusive proof of the rightness of Dr. Hort's theory; they could only belong to the region of hypothesis. **It is all hypothesis**. (my emphasis, HDW). I confess I feel strongly for myself that Dr. Hort's view represents the more probable side of the hypothesis, but at the same time I do not regard them standing alone as conclusive. I will end by venturing to do what Dr. Hort, with his great care and circumspection, has never done. It constantly seems as if his argument was leading up to it, but he never lets the name pass his lips. He thinks there was a revision of some kind; that is simply a way of describing the phenomena of the MSS on what appears to be the easiest hypothesis as to their origin. He thinks that a kind of revision took place at that time, and was a more or less continuous revision. I confess it has always seemed to me that that revision was probably connected with Lucian of Antioch and his school, which exercised great influence all through the fourth century. This type of text is prominent in his disciples, most prominent indeed in Theodore of Mopsuestia, where it reaches its culmination. The school was in close contact with the Syriac-speaking Churches and writers, and I have always suspected, although I cannot prove it, that this Traditional Text, of which Mr. Miller is so fond, owes its origin ultimately to Lucian of Antioch.

REV. G. H. GWILLIAM'S

RESPONDENT POSITON

FOR DEAN BURGON

(Editor's addition of the heading, HDW)

The **REV. G. H. GWILLIAM** (Fellow of Hertford) said:—I suppose I may as well, in the first place, declare on what side I am going to speak, although I shall not trouble you by entering very much into the question, as it has hitherto been discussed by Mr. Miller and the Margaret Professor. But I have not the least hesitation in standing up in support of Dean Burgon and Mr. Miller. It is very pleasant to cast aside labour and to disregard a number of MSS, confining oneself to a few. That is the principle of Lachmann, and is in fact what we are invited to do by the school of Dr. Hort. I shall not attempt to comment upon anything which has been said by the Margaret Professor, but I will express my surprise at one remark which fell constantly from his lips. Dr. Sanday constantly spoke of Aleph and B as if they agreed in text. I thought everybody knew they do not always agree, and therefore must not be brought as one authority. They are two discordant witnesses.

PROFESOR SANDAY (intervening):—May I be allowed to explain? What Mr. Gwilliam says is perfectly true, in regard to the agreement of Aleph and B. Dr. Hort laid stress upon their differences and quoted them as two authorities, but Mr. Miller is glad to quote them as only one. No doubt at a certain point Aleph and B had a common ancestor, and it is a question how near that ancestor was to the Autograph on the one hand and the actual MSS. on the other. I perfectly allow that there is a considerable amount of difference as well, but that tells in favour of Dr. Hort rather than against him.

MR. GWILLIAM:—I do not care in whose favor the difference tells; I want to arrive at the truth. I maintain that there is a difference between Aleph and B, and indeed between all the the oldest MSS; and I suppose it is in consequence of these differences that an appeal is to be made to the Versions. For if there were not these differences between the MSS I presume we might base our Text upon the Greek MSS only, and not appeal to translations at all. I think the importance of Versions may be exaggerated—I speak from my own point of view, and the Margaret Professor will not agree with me. When we have a mass of MSS handing down to us the Text of the New Testament, what occasion is there to go to the Latin or Egyptian, or what Dr. Sanday was courteous enough to call the sheet anchor of Mr. Miller's position, the Peshitto? This is a subject which demands considerable attention and is not one to be lightly treated in half an hour. Why should I speak? I would venture to remind you that I have already written upon the subject in several different publications, and it is a very significant circumstance that none has ever attempted to refute anything that I have said. The sensitiveness of some people about the Peshitto is very remarkable. Having occasion to write in the second volume of the *Studia Biblia,* which came out in 1890, on a certain Syriac subject, I made some remarks upon the value of the Peshitto. A certain member of the University said he should be very sorry for such remarks on the subject to issue from the Clarendon Press. In spite of that the remarks did issue and are extant to the present day. In the third volume of the *Studia Biblica* I more fully discussed the question; and I may venture to refer those who are interested in the subject to an article which I wrote upon subject to an article I wrote upon the same subject in the *Critical Review* for June, 1896. Lachman, I believe, said he did not know Syriac, and did not mean to study it. In that he was right, for the Greek MSS were quite enough for the settlement of the Text of the Greek Testament. Tregelles made a great mistake when he said the Syrians constantly revised their MSS. In co-operation with the late Philip Pusey I set to work to discover what the truth was, and found they did not so revise them. But there is a mass of evidence carrying the Syriac Text back to very early times, and supporting what the Margaret Professor has been kind enough to call the sheet anchor of the position. My friend, Mr. Crawford Burkitt, read a paper before the Church Congress at Norwich, and apologized in a private letter to me for being dogmatic, on the ground that he had not time to argue the question. I cannot allow dogmatism to be on one side. I accepted the apology, and in the same spirit I shall be extremely dogmatic now, for I cannot argue the question in five minutes, and I say that the Curetonian and Lewis MSS were not the origin of the Peshitto as we have it. The Margaret Professor spoke of them together as if they represented one kind of translation. If he would be so kind as to study a book which has been published by a certain gentleman I have the pleasure of seeing in this room, in which the two are compared, he will see that the Lewis and the Curetonian MSS were not two MSS of some one version which necessarily preceded the Peshitto. The Margaret Professor very pertinently referred to the principle of Dr. Hort, that to understand a text we must understand its history. We can know something of the history of the Peshitto. We have these many MSS and can collate them, and trace out the history, as Pusey and I have done. May I ask those who do not agree with me to remember that I have never said the Peshitto was not preceded by some other form of text.

All I say is that we have not got it now, and that the Lewis and Curetonian MSS were not the origin of the Peshitto. These things I state dogmatically, but I have stated the reasons and argued the point on previous occasions. It appears to me that the difference between my position and those who disagree with the late Philip Pusey and myself is this: They offer conjectures, while we offer arguments; they deal in surmises, while we collect and tabulate and set before the world facts.

The REV. A. C. HEADLAM:—May I ask what evidence Mr. Gwilliam can produce of the early date of the Peshitto, and how far back that evidence will carry it?

MR. GWILLIAM:—At least it carries us back to the fifth century, and it may be granted that the translation was not made before the second century. Have you any MSS of Sophocles which carry you back to the date of his original writings?

MR. ALLEN said:—In venturing to speak of the relation of the Lewis Codex and the Curetonian Syriac to the Peshitto I do so with the consciousness that I have not made that thorough and systematic examination of the material which alone can enable anyone to speak with authority upon a matter still under debate. But since, with hardly an exception, almost every writer who has discussed the question from the linguistic point of view has found reason to assert with some emphasis, that the internal evidence in favour of the priority of the Lewis and Curetonian MSS to the Peshitto is clear and unmistakable, I venture to restate some of the reasons for a position which my own slight acquaintance with the evidence persuades me is well grounded.

There is one point which I shall assume as proved because I do not know that anyone (Hilgenfeld alone excepted) has ever seriously disputed it. That is, that the Lewis Codex, the Curetonian, and the Peshitto are three recensions of one and the same version. This I imagine will hardly come within the scope of our consideration to-day. The point that this afternoon may be considered as still open, is the question whether the Lewis Codex and the Curetonian represent prior stages in the development of the Peshitto text, or whether they are corrupted recensions dependent upon it. The following are reasons for holding the former view. I have had occasion from time to time to make use of Mr. Bonus' valuable collation of the Lewis Codex with the Curetonian, and I have found reason to believe that the order in which the three recensions are placed upon his pages, the Lewis Codex first, the Curetonian in the middle, and the Peshitto last, can be justified as the historical order. The Curetonian gives us a text intermediate between the other two. As a test passage I have selected St. Matthew iv. 1-17, partly because the first twelve verses are discussed in Holzhey's monograph upon the subject, partly because I had previously worked through the same passage in my own note-books, and could therefore test my results by his.

I find that in these seventeen verses the Peshitto agrees with the Curetonian against the Lewis Codex about twenty-six times, with the Lewis against the Curetonian about thirteen times. That is to say, the Curetonian stands very much nearer to the Peshitto than does the Lewis Codex. Now is it possible that the right order is Peshitto, Curetonian, Lewis? or that the Curetonian and Lewis are two independent offshoots of the Peshitto? The latter hypothesis is precluded by the close verbal agreement of the Lewis and Curetonian against the Peshitto, the former by some cases where the Lewis Codex has a harsh or unexpected rendering which cannot be explained as an alteration of the Peshitto-Curetonian Text, but are intelligible if the Lewis Codex formed the first stage in the series. Such are verse 6, 'fall from hence,' altered by the Curetonian into 'cast thyself down,' in agreement with the Greek Text; 'arms' in the same verse, which in the Peshitto become 'hands;' v. 9, 'these kingdoms and their glory thou seest' altered in the Curetonian into 'all these things;' verse 16, 'in sadness and in the shadows of death,' of which the first word is omitted in Curetonian, and is changed in the Peshitto into an equivalent of the Greek χώρᾳ (chora).

It is of course difficult to prove much from a section of seventeen verses only, and I do not mean to say that difficulties do not sometimes arise which it is not easy to explain, the cases e. g. where the Peshitto and Lewis combine against the Curetonian. But every page of the Gospels confirms the impression made as it seems to me by the passage I have discussed that the Lewis Codex represents a prior stage in the Version, that it has been subjected to revision in the Curetonian, and that this again has been revised to harmonize with the Greek Text. And this might be supported by such considerations as that the Lewis Codex gives a much shorter text than that of the Curetonian, and that cases occur where renderings in Lewis which seem to be mistranslations of the Greek have been corrected either in the Curetonian and the Peshitto or in the latter only: e.g.

Matt. Xii. 25 εἰδὼς	L. C. 'saw'	P. 'knew'
John xviii. 4 εἰδὼς	L. 'saw'	P. 'knew'
Matt. Xviii.20 ου	L. 'not'	C. P. 'where'
Mark x.40 ἀλλ' οἷς	L. 'for others'	P.=GK
Luke iv. 29 κρημνίσαι	L. 'hang'	P. 'cast'
John vii. 35 διασποράν	L. C. 'seed'	P. 'places'

If I were discussing the question from a general point of view I should of course endeavour to support what has been said by the additional arguments, that the type of text found in the Lewis and Curetonian MSS. finds analogies in such early witnesses as the Diatessaron of Tatian and the quotations of Aphraates, further, that it often finds support in the earliest Greek MSS and in the Old Latin Versions; but arguments of this kind open up questions which are for this afternoon debatable ground, and which have been previously discussed.

In conclusion, I should like to say that the argument against the possibility of the Lewis Codex being a direct link in the development of the Peshitto Text, on the ground of the supposed heretical tendencies of its writer, seems to me unsound and dangerous. If it be true that truth precedes error, it is equally true that inaccurate and unguarded statement of truth has sometimes preceded the scientific expression of it. In a Version of the Gospels so accurate and careful as is the Lewis Codex, the few expressions with which fault has been found can at most have a colour of heresy when detached from their context and isolated. Until we have further evidence which will force us to conclude that the scribe of this codex was heretically inclined, it seems to be more reasonable to look upon these expressions as primitive methods of expression which were afterwards modified. Of course I do not mean that they give us the true reading, but only that they represent a very early stage in the history of the *Syriac* Text, and that to urge that the Lewis Codex is a corrupted recension of the Peshitto on dogmatic grounds is to misread the evidence. Even if in such case it is certain that the Peshitto retains the true reading and the Lewis Codex a corrupted one, it may still be true that as far as the Syriac Versions are concerned the Lewis Codex presents us with an earlier form of text which has been modified in the Peshitto to harmonize with the Greek Text.

Psalms 100:5 "For the LORD *is* good; his mercy *is* everlasting; and his truth *endureth* to all generations."

REV. A. BONUS RESPONDENT

FOR DEAN BURGON

(Editor's addition of the heading, HDW)

The REV. A. BONUS (Pembroke): In the very short time allowed me I can only make a few brief observations. Referring for a moment to what has just been said, I should like to point out that in the places where the Lewis and Curetonian MSS differ, the latter agree or tend to agree with the Peshitto in SS. Matthew and John many more times than Lewis agrees or tends to agree with the Peshitto in the same Gospels; whereas in St Luke the respective agreements or tendencies to agreement between Cureton and the Peshitto, and between Lewis and the Peshitto, are fairly equal. This is a remarkable circumstance, which demands careful attention. Connected with this there is another point of interest. Lewis, as you are aware, is characterized in parts by the use of the word 'Lord' instead of the word 'Jesus.' This is the case in St. Matthew, and especially in St. John—I am speaking of course of those parts only of Lewis and Cureton which are available for comparison— but in St. Luke the case seems reversed. Thus, whilst in St. Matthew and St. John Lewis inclined to the use of 'Lord' and Cureton to the use of 'Jesus,' in St. Luke Lewis inclined to the use of 'Jesus' and Cureton to the use of 'Lord.' These, and some other kindred facts which my collation of the Syriac Gospels brought before me, are important. Do they not indicate that the texts of Lewis and of Cureton are not homogeneous, or at least that they have been subjected to a varying textual influence?

Turning to the Peshitto problem, I should like to say in a few words how the case seems to me to stand. It is generally allowed—I believe by Dr. Sanday among others—that MSS and quotations carry back our knowledge of the Peshitto roughly speaking to the beginning of the fourth century, say for convenience A.D. 310; and the question is how and when did it come into existence. It would appear that there were, speaking broadly, only two alternatives containing four possibilities—revision or translation. It might then have been the result of the revision of previously existing Syriac texts—a revision conducted gradually, without anyone authority; a revision extending over a long period of time, until at last the Peshitto, as we know it, was evolved. The objection to this theory seems to be that there are no traces of such a revision; if such a process has been gone through, it is next to certain that there will be extensive traces of it in the Peshitto MSS—traces of irregular revision and of mixture. And if anyone says, 'Well, you have the antecedents of the Peshitto in Lewis and Cureton,' that is not the point. The point is that no Peshitto MS. shows any signs of mixture or of irregular revision; for Mr. Gwilliam and the late Mr. Pusey appear to be quite correct in saying that the variations between Peshitto MSS are insignificant and are largely only slight changes in grammatical forms. This appears to be the place to remark that I cannot understand how anyone can suppose, in the language of Dr. Hort, that 'the Syriac Version, like the Latin Version, underwent revision long after its origin.' The facts seem scarcely at all parallel In the case of the Latin there is historical evidence of revision; in the case of the Peshitto none. In the case of the Latin there are in existing MSS abundant traces of sporadic and casual mixture, and of irregular revision; there is nothing of the kind in the Peshitto MS.

PROFESSOR SANDAY (intervening):—Nobody has ever contended that the Peshitto itself was revised, except in the later forms of the Version known as the Philoxenian and Harclean, but that it was the product of a revision. An analogous case is that of Codex Brixianus and a small group of Latin authorities, which go far to show that there was a revision of the Latin Version before the time of Jerome, of which nothing is known historically.[31]

MR. BONUS :—Of course, where everything is in the dark we can suppose anything. Turning to the second possibility under the first alternative, the Peshitto may be the outcome of an authoritative revision of the Syriac Text. This appears to be Dr. Hort's view, and Dr. Hort seems inclined to suppose that it may have taken place not far from 300 A.D., that is soon after the supposed first Syrian (Greek) revision. I have always felt that there were at least two formidable objections to this theory, for while fully recognizing the precariousness of arguing from silence, it is certainly hard to understand, if such an authoritative revision had taken place at so comparatively late a date, why no notice was taken of it by Syriac writers. Nor is there merely the difficulty of accounting for the silence of Syriac writers as to any such definite revision, but there is the further difficulty—supposing such a revision had been made—of accounting for their silence as to any authoritative removal of 'old Syriac' Texts and the imposition of the revised Text on the Syriac Churches, and on the supposition of a definite authoritative revision something of this kind must have taken place. We are told of the removal of Tatian's work, and of the Philoxenian revision. Why are we not told of this important change? The argument from silence must no doubt be used with caution, but under the circumstances a 'consensus of silence,' as some one has phrased it, deserves serious consideration. The first possibility of the

---

[31] This explanation was not expressed quite accurately at the time, but is given here in the form which it should have taken.

second alternative is that the Peshitto may be a direct translation made from the Greek somewhere about 300 A. D., that is soon after Dr. Hort's supposed first Syriac (Greek) revision, and based upon that revision. But the objections to the previous suppositions apply with equal force to this. Lastly, there is the possibility that the Peshitto is a direct translation from the Greek made at a time long anterior to 300 A.D., at a time that is to say when literary and ecclesiastical activity in the Syriac Churches was, by comparison with that of a later age, feeble, when, in the language of Canon Cook, 'such a transaction might have escaped notice or have been passed over as of slight historical importance, not bearing upon the external organization of the Church, or upon controversies which occupied almost exclusively the minds-of its chief representatives.' In conclusion, the only reasonable interpretation of the evidence—largely negative and inferential, no doubt—seems to be that the Peshitto, whether it were the result of revision or whether it were a direct translation from the Greek, must have come into existence long before the beginning of the fourth century—scarcely later than the latter half of the second century. But if this were so, the Greek text on which it was based must have existed at or before that date. I may add that I quite admit that Texts like those of Lewis or Cureton may have existed in the second century, but even if it were beyond doubt that Aphraates and Tatian used only such Texts that would be no evidence that the Peshitto Text did not exist when either of those writers lived. We could merely argue that if the Peshitto then existed it was not in the proper sense of the word a Vulgate.

REV. A. C. HEADLAM OPPONENT

AGAINST DEAN BURGON

(Editor's addition of the heading, HDW)

The REV. A. C. HEADLAM (All Souls) said.—I have worked for a considerable time in some small portions of the Bible on Textual Criticism, and I have always done so, as far as I could, with my eyes open and with a great desire not to be prejudiced in favour of anyone theory; but I have found the more I have tested them the stronger the arguments of Westcott and Hort have seemed to appear. There are certain definite scientific arguments which they used, and I have read writers on the other side, and have tried in vain to find them answered, but I have rarely found them even understood. That is of course only giving my own impression. There is one line upon which I am quite unable to follow the arguments, and that is upon the relative dates of the Peshitto and the Curetonian. Mr. Gwilliam and others constantly asserted that all the arguments were against Westcott and Hort. I have listened with great care to what has been said to-day, and I particularly asked Mr. Gwilliam for the evidence of the early date of the Peshitto. ,I saw at once that the evidence he quoted was perfectly useless. He told us his evidence dated back as far as the fifth century, and argued that therefore it must go back to the second, further saying that there was a clear Text without any sign of mixture. Upon referring to the earliest Texts of the Vulgate you will find those Texts possess hardly any signs of mixture. Mixture means that a Text has grown up and had a long history. If in the fifth century there were a considerable number of MSS of the Peshitto which agreed in a remarkable manner, that shows almost conclusively that the Texts must have been derived from one source, which could not have been very remote. A common argument used with regard to the Gospels is that the extraordinary variety of Texts which confront us, oblige us to throw back the composition of the documents to a very early stage. Mr. Gwilliam's argument compels me to think that the Peshitto must be of a comparatively recent date, and must come from an authoritative edition. I have also listened carefully to Mr. Bonus' argument. It is admitted on both sides that we might go back to the beginning of the fourth century. We want some evidence to connect the Peshitto with an earlier period. If you are going to make that document any evidence at all to overthrow Dr. Hort's conclusions, you must show conclusively that it existed at an earlier period. You cannot overthrow a body of statements built up on a groundwork of facts by mere surmises. That is exactly the position in which we are with regard to the Syriac. I have tried to find any arguments which would tell against Westcott and Hort, and I find that practically Mr. Gwilliam and Mr. Bonus repeat statements which Westcott and Hort would be the very first to admit. I had hoped that the discussion would turn upon further interesting questions which have lately arisen. Dr. Salmon's book on Textual Criticism brings us to this position—he criticizes Westcott and Hort, but practically accepts the great contention which separates him from Mr. Miller; he accepts in some form or other the Antiochene revision, though, like Professor Sanday and Dr. Hort himself, he does not think it was quite such a formal revision as some of those who attack the theory think. He then tries to find out whether in certain points the authority of the Western Text cannot be set up. That is really the point at issue before scholars at the present day, whether the Western Text does not really contain some considerable element of truth. Personally I cannot think it does.

Various attempts which have been put forward to set up that Text have failed almost entirely in the main argument, but this much is true, that occasionally as it gives independent tradition it will contain readings which are possibly true, and may help us to correct in certain points the readings of the other group. But it will do so probably as against the Traditional Text, and not in its favour. That is the conclusion I have arrived at from a careful study of portions of St. Paul's Epistles. Here I may add that Dr. Sanday did not refer to the fact that the conclusion we came to with regard to one MS 'B,' was that we ought to be very careful in using it, because it was found that from time to time the MS had been exposed, especially in the Epistles, to certain corrupt influences. As a matter of fact, sometimes when the MS stands quite alone and is unsupported by any other authorities, it gives a reading which in some small point, where one would hardly expect it to occur, was that which in all probability was an original reading. One has to be very cautious indeed about taking a reading upon the authority of a single MS, but sometimes we feel inclined to do so. Mr. Miller has asked the question what the classical scholar would do when face to face with the mass of evidence contained in the New Testament. We happen to know what a classical scholar has done. Dr. Blass came as a classical scholar to the study of the New Testament and of the Acts of the Apostles. The very first thing he did was to sweep away a whole mass of later authorities, saying that to a classical student like himself, coming to such good authorities as the New Testament was preserved in, it seemed perfectly useless to consider those later authorities which clearly contained a mixed text. As a matter of fact, in the case of most classical texts now, authorities have discovered that the mass of MSS. are derived from one single authority, and it is very rarely indeed that any attention is paid to the great majority of them.

Psalms 119:152 "Concerning thy testimonies, I have known of old that thou hast founded them for ever."

PREBENDARY MILLER'S

SUMMATION

(Editor's addition of the heading, HDW)

PREBENDARY MILLER:—I have only a very few words to say in reply. With respect to the last remark, I think what Dr. Blass did can hardly be justified. It is quite true that that is what a classical scholar has done, but it is surely throwing away evidence which he has no right to do. You might easily go to another scholar, Lachmann, who did the same. They have thought it impossible to deal with so much evidence. It seems to me that it is a very poor reason for casting away a great quantity of evidence because it is beyond your powers to deal with it in one age. Turning to the other point, the Peshitto, it is very curious that there should be such a difference between those who think the Peshitto came from the first, and those who say they cannot find any evidence to show that such was the case. We trace it back in line of evidence. It occurs in the readings of Aphraates and Ephraem Syrus according to accounts, but there is no time to argue the question now. I would rather refer to an article in the *Church Quarterly* and to a chapter in my first volume. But there is one thing I think ought to be borne in mind, that the Peshitto has not got the ἀντιλεγόμενα (antiligomena) or books once not universally received, and that is a very strong reason for supposing that the translation from the Greek took place at a very early date—indeed, before those books were generally in use.[32] I think I said we hold there was no authoritative

---

[32] Edward Miller must be referring to the Apocrypha, which was universally rejected, but it was included in Origen's LXX in the

revision of the Greek, but that the revision merely grew by itself. With respect to Μονογενὴς Θεός (Monogenes Theos), my views have been put forth in my second volume to which Dr. Sanday referred. That reading we hold was introduced by Valentinus for heretical purposes, and it is no credit to these MSS to bring it forward. Again, he said that history as it is presented by us was an afterthought. Let me say, that as far as I am concerned, that is in no wise the case.[33] There was another difficulty, you will all remember, in our argument. We were obliged to argue against a great number of scholars, to whose eminence, ability, and knowledge I wish to pay the greatest tribute. Both those volumes are necessarily argumentative. That is not a case where you are so likely to make limitations and look in a wider and more conciliatory way. I hope therefore that this consideration will be remembered when any attention is turned to that point. I am very much surprised to find that Dr. Sanday says that Conflation is not a process running through the Gospels. It is quite true Westcott and Hort do not actually say so, but there is great prominence given to Conflation in their work. I expect Dr. Sanday has been guided very much by his own experience of it, and has come to the conclusion that it does not go very far. I am quite sure anybody reading Dr. Hort's book will infer that it holds a very integral place in his theory, and is very important in that theory. I do not think it can be justified, and I am delighted to feel that Dr. Sanday agrees with me upon this point. I do not think it is necessary, after all the argument we have had to discuss further the subject.[34]

Hexapla and subsequent copies of it called the Septuagint. (HDW)

[33] I made an ineffectual attempt in 1882 to review Westcott and Hort's theory mainly from an historical point of view, and the historical part of my 'Textual Guide' was singled out for special praise by Dean Burgon, whose own arguments have much that is historical in them.

[34] Mr. Miller intended to add more remarks, but was prevented

Matthew 5:17-18 "Think not that I am come to destroy the law, or the prophets: I am not come to destroy, but to fulfil. [18] For verily I say unto you, Till heaven and earth pass, one jot or one tittle shall in no wise pass from the law, till all be fulfilled."

---

by the inexorable approach of the College dinner-hour which indeed curtailed his reply throughout. Inevitable limits of time hampered all the speakers.

The

Traditional Text of the Holy

Gospels,

VINDICATED AND ESTABLISHED.

VOLUME II.

The Causes of the Corruption

in the

Traditional Text of the Holy

Gospels.

BY THE LATE

JOHN WILLIAM BURGON, B.D.,

DEAN OF CHICHESTER

Arranged, Completed. and Edited by EDWARD MILLER, M.A., Wykehamical Prebendary
of Chichester Cathedral; Author of 'A Guide to the Textual Criticism of the New
Testament.'

TO BE HAD SEPARATELY.

LONDON: GEORGE BELL &: SONS.
CAMBRIDGE: DEIGHTON, BELL &: CO.

Psalms 119:160 "Thy word *is* true *from* the beginning: and every one of thy righteous judgments *endureth* for ever."

INDEX

www.ingramcontent.com/pod-product-compliance
Lightning Source LLC
Chambersburg PA
CBHW060134050426
42448CB00010B/2116